ALBANIA
A TRAVEL GUIDE

D1355576

ALBANIA
A TRAVEL GUIDE

Philip Ward

THE OLEANDER PRESS

The Oleander Press
17 Stansgate Avenue
Cambridge CB2 2QZ
England

Hippocrene Books, Inc.
171 Madison Avenue
New York
N.Y. 10016
U.S.A.

British Library Cataloguing in Publication Data

Ward, Philip
    Albania: a travel guide.—(Oleander travel books series;
    v. 10)
    1. Albania—Description and travel
    —Guide books
    I. Title
    914.96′5043   DR909
    ISBN 0-906672-41-4
    ISBN 0-906672-42-2 Pbk

Designed by Ron Jones

Typeset, printed and bound in Great Britain

Contents

MAP OF ALBANIA

TIRANË

DURRES	POPULATION
DURRES	+150,000
BERAT	30,000–100,000
Krujë	10,000–30,000
Peqin	6,000–10,000

TIRANË Capital city

DURRES District capital

National boundary

District boundary

Railway

Motorable roads

Air route

Port

Airport

Sea route

AMANTIA Classical sites, with their classical names

ALB

Tourist sites

Tourist routes

Seaside resorts

43 km Distances in km

Metres above sea level
2400
1800
1200
600
300
100

Metres below sea level
50
100
500
6,000

0   8   16 km

List of Illustrations

Preface

Time spent in Albania may be considered more of an adventure than a holiday, for the physical difficulty of reaching the border through Belgrade and Montenegrin Titograd is more than matched by the intellectual leap from a modern capitalist state of Western Europe to the last remaining hard-line Communist state of Eastern Europe where statues and portraits of Stalin—not to mention his published works—are everywhere visible.

In June 1980 the estimated population of Albania was 2,670,000, 96.95% being Albanians; ethnic minorities were 2.54% Greeks, 0.41% Yugoslavs, and 0.10% others. The last census (January 1979) gave a total population of 2,591,000. The area of Albania is 28,748 sq.km., or 11,100 sq.miles.

Officially, the Head of State is Haxhi Lleshi, who took office in 1953. Full members of the Politburo of the Central Committee of the Party of Labour early in 1981 were R. Alia, A. Carcani, K. Hasbiu, E. Hoxha, H. Isai, S. Koleka, R. Marko, P. Miska, H. Myftiu and H. Toska.

Be prepared for the same mental adjustment to Albanian nationalism that you would make to Burmese Buddhism or to Syrian Islam, or do not travel to Albania. The attitude shown throughout this book tries to steer a middle course between a naive defence of monolithic Albanianism and a naive attack. A sycophantic approach is in some ways as insulting as a mocking or scornful attitude, for both take an easy way out by accepting a party line or rejecting it out of hand. No: *Albania: a Travel Guide* is by a Briton with no axe to grind and no preconceptions to support. It has been written for the independently-minded who care to look behind the Adriatic Curtain. Albania is an intrinsically fascinating state which boasts very little crime and suffers very little freedom of action outside the strict confines of puritanical morality. A state where at least officially nobody is unemployed and nobody is rich. Where road accidents are virtually unknown because there are so few vehicles, and because nobody may own a private car. Where miles and miles of golden beaches cannot be overcrowded because there are insufficient hotels.

1

It could be fairly argued that the present Albanian regime is responsible for a number of spectacular successes, and a number of spectacular failures. On the credit side are literacy, basic health, law and order, and the improvement of conditions for women and children. On the debit side are education (understood in its higher sense of broadening the mind), leisure, the material standard of living, civil liberties, and a failure to check the increase of bureaucracy, especially during the worst years of 1966–72, openly criticised by Comrade Enver himself.

I stress that I visited Albania in May–June 1982 as an anonymous member of an ordinary tour, and was given no special privilege of any kind, but paid my own way and asked no favours. It follows that anyone else going on a similar group tour will be offered exactly the same facilities, though Regent Holidays (U.K.) Ltd do suggest that you state your special interests in advance, so that Albturist may arrange a visit to a school or factory, artist's studio or agricultural co-operative. Our own group visited a textile factory, a kindergarten, state farms in the centre and south of the country and (in subgroups) a public library, a film show, a meeting with a High Court Judge, two theatres, and a meeting with a poet and the Editor-in-Chief of *Drita*, the leading cultural weekly paper. Even if opportunities for evening entertainment are not offered by the Albturist guides, energetic group members may prospect for local evening performances on arrival, and put these suggestions to the guides.

As well as Naim Distafa, English-language chief of Albturist, I thank for assistance in Albania the Albturist guides Flora and Lejla and our driver Koço; Zihni Sako; Bardhyl Londo and Xhevat Lloshi; Ardian Cerga and the rest of the outstanding cast of *Dy krisma në Paris*; and all the many helpful and courteous Albanians who made our adventure so enjoyable. In England I acknowledge with gratitude the help given by Stuart Mann, Martin Coombs, Phil Tompsett, Anton Logoreci, Neil Taylor, Colin Flegg, Gillian Ely, Ron Jones, and the staffs of Cambridgeshire Libraries and Cambridge University Library. William Bland of the Albanian Society was particularly generous in offering his time for discussion, and the loan of the *Spoken Albanian* textbook and accompanying cassettes. My wife Audrey and my daughters Carolyn and Angela have given me the time and space to work in serenity: whatever virtue these pages may have is attributable to their loving influence, while the shortcomings are all my own.

Chronology of Albania

B.C.

100,000—10,000	Middle and Late Paleolithic
5000	Neolithic (e.g. Cakran settlement on the south coast)
2700—1200	Neolithic Maliq settlement near Korçë
627	Colonisation of coast (Epidamnos, now Durrës; Apollonia) by Greeks from Corfu
385	Dionysius of Syracuse rules from Lezhë
297	Pyrrhus (killed 272) leads Epirotic League
232	Epidamnos taken by the Illyrian leader Glaukias, who allies himself with Rome and makes city (now Dyrrachium) the port for the Roman Via Egnatia to Constantinople
229—168	Roman invasions establish province of Illyricum
49	First Civil War between Pompey and Caesar

A.D.

395	Illyricum divided between Eastern and Western Roman Empires
c.520	First (Byzantine) fortress of Tirana
529—640	Invasions by Antes, Huns, Lombards, Gepides, Slavs and Avars
645	Byzantine Church of Lin, near Pogradec
c.840	Byzantine dominion re-established
851	Bulgars begin invasions
1014	Basil II retakes Albania for Byzantium
c.1050	Church and Monastery of Mesopotamos, near Sarandë

1081	Bohemond leads Normans to invade Durrës from Italy
1096	Armies of the First Crusade devastate Albania
1109	Normans withdraw
1190–8	Feudal state of 'Arbania' under Progon, with its capital at Krujë
1272–86	Roman Catholicism introduced by Charles of Anjou into the Regnum Albaniae (Northern Albania)
1331–55	Serbian dominion under Stefan Dušan
1366–1421	Balsha dynasty
1385–1417	Sultan Murad I invades Albania
1405?–68	Gjergj Kastrioti, called Skënderbeg, resists Ottoman invasions from his capital of Krujë
1466–7	Sultan Mehmet rebuilds fortress of Elbasan as a stronghold from which to seize Krujë
1474	Krujë sold to Venetians by Skënderbeg's son
1506–1912	Ottoman Empire subdues all Albania
1726	Church of St Nicholas, Voskopojë
1741–1822	Ali Pasha of Tepelenë rules South Albania and Epirus as a fief from the Porte
1750–1831	Bushatli dynasty in North Albania
1796–7	Mosque of Ethem Bey, Tirana
1813–1903	Girolamo de Rada, leading poet and propagandist for Albanianism in Italy
1846–1900	Naim Frashëri, leading political and literary figure in Albanian renaissance
1854	Albanian Cultural Association founded at Bucharest
1866	Publication of *Scanderbeg* by de Rada
1878	League of Prizren (from 10 June)
1881	Turkish army occupies Prizren and dissolves League
1887	First Albanian-language school opens at Korçë
1912	National Government formed at Vlorë (28 November)

1913	London Conference (29 July) recognises Albania's independence and creates (roughly speaking) the modern boundaries
1914	Government of Prince Wilhelm von Wied (7 March–3 September). Greek forces occupy Vlorë (December)
1915	Montenegrin forces occupy Shkodër (June)
1916	Korçë declared 'autonomous province' (December) ruled by Albanians under French military protection (ended February 1918)
1919	Anti-Italian demonstrations at Vlorë (November)
1920	Congress of Lushnjë (21 January) provides new Constitution. League of Nations admits Albania (27 December)
1920–4	Administration of Fan Noli
1921	Ambassadors' Conference, Paris, readjusts boundaries (November)
1923	Population census: 817,460. London Conference proclaims Albania an autonomous principality
1924	Avni Rustemi (murderer of Esat Pasha Toptani) is himself killed (20 April). Ahmet Zogu seizes Tirana (14 December)
1925–8	President Zog rules with Italian support
1928–39	King Zog I rules with Italian support
1939	King Zog flees (8 April) the day after Italian forces invade. Italian occupation
1941	Albanian Communist Party founded (8 November). First Party Conference (ends 14 November)
1943	German occupation (11 September to 29 November 1944)
1944	First National Liberation and Anti-Fascist Congress at Përmet (24 May). Communists seize power (29 November). Period of Yugoslav influence (to September 1948)
1945	First general election (2 December) won by the only permitted party, the Communists
1948–60	Period of Soviet influence

1951–5	First Five-Year Plan
1956–60	Second Five-Year Plan
1957	University of Tirana established
1961–5	Third Five-Year Plan
1961–78	Period of Chinese influence
1966–70	Fourth Five-Year Plan
1971–5	Fifth Five-Year Plan
1975	Population census: 2,430,000 (having tripled in 52 years)
1976	Change of Constitution
1976–80	Sixth Five-Year Plan
1978–	Period of international isolationism
1981–5	Seventh Five-Year Plan
1981	Albania becomes world's second largest exporter of chrome. Death of Mehmet Shehu
1982	H. Lleshi replaced as nominal Head of State by R. Alia, and major ministerial reshuffle (November)

1
The Adventure Starts

The Jugoslavenski Aerotransport DC-9 which took off from Heathrow to Zagreb at midday included a group of twenty-five people on their indirect way to Albania. Perhaps one could judge from the faces which were the passengers on Albturist/82/3, paying £370.19 for a general tour of Albania in May and June. One ruled out the Yugoslavs, the English couples with 'Yugotours' tags on their hand-baggage, and considered the rest. Yes: there were the Regent Holidays (UK) Ltd. tags, on flight-bags carried by an Australian secretary from Darwin, a fruit-farmer from Kent, a solicitor from Newcastle, a carpenter from London, a Muslim community supervisor from Blackburn, an education officer and his wife from Surrey, a librarian from Tamworth. The ages ranged from 19 (Lucy from Kensington) to 76 (John from Harrow), but their political involvement was not so varied: though all started with open minds, most at least were relieved to return to the outside world from 'Tibet-in-Europe', a country which has preferred isolation to the joining of any power bloc.

The group leader, Colin Flegg, a data analyst from Bristol, explained that there would be several hours delay at Zagreb Airport before the connecting flight to Titograd in Montenegro, and most of us took the chance to explore the second city of Yugoslavia, taking the airport bus 17km. to the city centre. Four years ago I had spent several memorable days in Zagreb, lodging with Mrs Marcelja at Brace Kavurica 7/II, and I had enjoyed the Lievens, Donatello and Fra Angelico in the Strossmayer, and the Gallery of Naive Painters in which Yugoslavia is particularly rich. One evening I had seen *Tosca* sung by Blaženka Milić, Krunoslav Cigoj, and Duško Kukovec, and conducted by Miro Belamarić; and another, also at the elegant Croatian National Theatre, Flemming Flindt's new ballet *The Three Musketeers*.

Now I felt like revisiting St Mark's in the Radićev Trg. Though the brilliantly-tiled roof is as recent as nineteenth-century in date, most of the surviving church dates from the fourteenth to fifteenth centuries. The whole of the surrounding square is picturesque in the Central and Eastern

European styles from Vienna and Krakow to Weimar and Prague. One mingles with people in the square who might have modelled for the modern frescoes of Kljaković in St Mark's.

Late in the evening another DC-9 flew us from Zagreb to Sarajevo and from Sarajevo to Titograd, the modern city which has replaced bombed Podgorica. We stayed at the only good hotel in Titograd, the Podgorica; opposite is the Hotel Crna Gora named for the Black Mountains which gives 'Montenegro' its familiar western name.

The following morning our group assembled for conveyance to the Yugoslav border. The road narrows out of Titograd, revealing how little traffic passes between the two countries. We were made to throw our baggage open for a cursory customs inspection by the side of the road, and then walked to the Albanian barrier, carrying out own bags. Below us frogs yammered among the water-lilies by the edge of Lake Shkodër, hopping illicitly between Yugoslavia and Albania as if they were smuggling croaks. Our passports were solemnly handed over with our group visa, and one by one, like candidates entering an examination room before strict and suspicious armed invigilators, we filed through the barrier and in the warm morning by Lake Shkodër baptised our shoes in a disinfectant pool in the middle of the road and headed for the Albanian border reception room, to be greeted by a pretty Albturist courier called Flora, who was to stay with us throughout. In comfortable armchairs we again displayed our changes of underwear and sponge-bags to the interested inspection of ambulant customs officers. On the walls the portrait of Comrade Enver Hoxha stared stonily at strange Albanian souvenirs in a glass-case, and editions of Comrade Enver's works in many languages were propped up mutely in locked bookcases facing colour photographs of Comrade Enver, and an English-language statement by Comrade Enver which warned any potential subversives among us:

EVEN IF WE HAVE TO GO WITHOUT BREAD,
WE ALBANIANS DO NOT VIOLATE PRINCIPLES.
WE DO NOT BETRAY MARXISM-LENINISM.

The Albanian authorities are quite convinced that every tourist group conceals the presence of an undercover agent of the CIA, KGB, MI5 or the British and Foreign Bible Society. I wondered uneasily if the four Muslims among us were hiding Korans in their flowing garments, or whether the quiet architect from East London was a secret Mormon evangelist. Regent Holidays had spelled out a number of Albanian fears: 'Citizens of the U.S.A. are not permitted entry, nor persons employed as journalists. No male with long hair or full beard will be allowed into the country. A beard is permitted providing there is a large shaven area between sideboards and start of beard. Should the authorities not be satisfied in this respect, hair will be cut by the barber on arrival.'

There is thus an official dread of a shaggy American reporter wearing bright clothes, his baggage stuffed with Bibles and contraceptives. It is not clear whether anyone answering to that description would in any case wish to enter Albania, but the phobias of other people are always intriguing. The ideological emphasis of the waiting-room ensures that we are in no doubt as to the danger of committing an unspeakable insult by speaking ill of Comrade Enver, though the line taken throughout is that he is simply the Secretary of the Party of Labour and has no kind of special presidential or prime-ministerial status. This is puzzling in view of the fact that virtually all of the tens of thousands of hoardings and banners throughout Albania make some reference to him, and his is the only photograph in shops, offices, and hotels. In many places the bare mountainside has been carved with a slogan like PARTI ENVER (Enver's Party), and his works take pride of place in every bookshop.

We filled in our Custom-House Declaration, or rather enquiry: 'Do You posses any of the goods mentioned below, Transmiter and receiver radio sets, Camera Recorder, Television set, Refrigarator, Washing machine and other house commodities, Watches, Drugs, Priuted matter such as letters, Books Magazines, Different currencies, explosives.' All innocent of Washing machine, priuted letters and explosives, we felt immune to prosecution, even though—as the form went on to explain—'Goods which are not declared to the customhouse are cousidered as smuglling, smugglers will be punished according to the law'. There was nowhere to change money, and it is forbidden to import leks, so the sign 'café' in the customs-house was more of a provocation than an invitation.

Formalities completed, we trooped on to the shining new Italian-made Menarini coach, air-conditioned and as comfortable as any on the market. We cruised slowly along the poor roads, hardly improved since they were maintained by the Azienda Strade Albania set up in 1939. There are no motorways in Albania, and even the ubiquitous locally-produced bitumen does not seem to be used adequately. The main reason is that the roads are not really exploited by motor-traffic in the Western European sense of the term, for there are no privately-owned cars, and the huge majority of vehicles are tough Chinese and Russian trucks built to cope with roads far worse than these. There is no spare-parts problem, with a spare-parts factory in Tirana, and a machine-tool factory to ensure that the traffic does not stop. If you do see cars, the Mercedes Benz is the prerogative of top officials, the Volvo of the second echelon, and the Fiat of the third.

While the bus racketed along, Flora welcomed us to Albania and asked us to obey only two restrictions on photography: no military buildings, sites or objects, such as ports or bunkers;' and nobody in military uniform, such as soldiers. In fact, I should advise that you never take a photograph of anyone without asking their permission first, since there are so few foreigners that you may still cause embarrassment in country districts. And since the hundreds of thousands of camouflaged bunkers are dotted around town parks as well as roads and hillsides, be very careful not to offend the Albanian couriers and drivers who may ultimately be answerable to the authorities for a tourist's thoughtless snap.

Midway along the 34km. Shkodër road from the border at Han i Hotit to Shkodër is the little village of Lower Koplik (Cinna in classical times), set in an agricultural plain. Our first night in Albania was to be spent at Shkodër (Shkodra with the definite article), but first we were to visit the Fortress of Rozafat high above. While the party changed for the outing I took heed of Thoreau's saying 'It is a great art to saunter', and explored the main square of Shkodër. I suppose the first impression of any Westerner in an Albanian town, from Kukës to Sarandë, is the eerie silence of traffic-free roads. Many times I caught myself looking left, right, and left again, and seeing no car, motor-bike or even cycle, but only a cluster of small boys, or a couple of factory workers crossing the street. Traffic policemen in the larger towns, identifiable in the brightest blue that Albanians will wear, resort to whistling at jay-walkers. Opposite the Hotel Rozafat there is an artist's rendering of what traffic rules one should obey in the event of any traffic, and this too attracts the casual interest of saunterers like myself. So does the absence of names on shop-fronts, instead of the terse BUKË, LIBRARI, or USHQIMORË (respectively BREAD, BOOKSHOP, FOODSTORE). As if to turn topsy-turvy all we had ever read of the people's selling all their goods and services through the state system, I strolled the gauntlet of silent women, wrapped up against the street-dust, kneeling, crouching, or sitting cross-legged on the pavement, with one hand opening to reveal as I passed one egg, or a tiny basket of greens, or even a metal cross. One old woman looked about to die of sorrow, her damp eyes full of so many tragedies that they had turned to commonplace black stone.

A single-decker bus lurched past, crowded to the doors with factory workers. An uncomplaining donkey hitched up to a cart was dozing in the cruel sun.

The ex-Roman Catholic Cathedral on the main street is now a sports hall, and a former convent is believed to be the headquarters of the secret

Shkodër. Street scene.

Shkodër. Former Roman
Catholic Cathedral, now a
sports hall.

police, but this is impossible for a foreigner to verify. Vatican Radio announced in April 1969 that a Roman Catholic priest, Father Shkurti, had escaped over the Yugoslav border with several of his parishioners but the Yugoslav authorities had handed them back, and Father Shkurti had been executed by firing squad on 26 November 1968 (*The Daily Telegraph*, 23 April 1969).

Seeing the terrified, mangy cats in the streets of Shkodër I recalled Nirad Chaudhuri's words in *A Passage to England.* 'I observed that the stray cats which were going to their day-shelters did not slink down or take cover under motor-cars [as they do in his native Delhi] when they see a man, but walked on with *insouciance*, with a glance of mild curiosity at me. Soon they began to make direct overtures. At Canterbury, when I was walking among the ruins of St Augustine's Abbey, a cat came up and rolled on the path before me, in order to be picked up and tickled under the chin.' Chaudhuri says later that cats are 'very good judges of human character, and all nations get the cats they deserve.' Throughout the Middle East and Far East, generally speaking, cats are treated as vermin. In Albania, too, it is not uncommon to see small boys walking along with a pebble in their hand to throw at a cat, and cats are lucky if they locate a hotel or restaurant whose garbage area they haunt for scraps. Dogs are kept less for companionship than for use, as an occasional watchdog (at a house I saw near a mosque on Krujë castle, for instance) and a rare sheepdog. But few Albanians keep pets at all, and the streets of cities remain dusty but unfouled.

I found the garden of the Folk Museum (Muzeu Popullor) open, though the museum itself was sleeping the siesta of all Middle Eastern museums. Half-hearted classical columns propped themselves anonymously against a wall and the well, while a forlorn Ottoman gravestone leaned obliquely into the wind of history. I noted the times of opening of all the museums in Shkodër: the Folk Museum (devoted to history and ethnography) from 10–12 on Wednesdays, Thursdays, Saturdays and Sundays, and from 6–8 on Thursdays, Saturdays and Sundays; the House and Museum of the Three Heroes (communists, who resisted the Italian Occupation, named Kadia, Misja, and Rexhepi), from 6–8 on Tuesdays and Thursdays; the House and Museum of the local patriot Luigj Gurakuqi (1879–1925), from 6–8 on Wednesdays and Sundays; and the House and Museum of the local author 'Migjeni', from 6–8 on Wednesdays and Sundays. Gurakuqi opened two hundred elementary schools under the Austrian régime during World War I, having been appointed the first Albanian Minister of Education in 1912. 'Migjeni' was the pen-name of the precocious novelist Milosh Gjergj Nikolla (1909–38), who composed the poems collected as *Kanga Lirije*

(Songs of Freedom) but remains best known for his autobiographical novel *Luli i Vocërr* (Little Luli).

The museum which you will be taken to see is the Muzeu Ateist (Atheist Museum, open 10–12 and 6–8 on Mondays, Wednesdays, Saturdays and Sundays), in a pleasant square off the main street not far from an excellent ice-cream parlour. As in all Albanian museums, the displays tend to be didactic in a tiresomely old-fashioned way, and in a country determined that only one ideology shall be given a hearing, pluralists from the West may become restive. There are two floors, with captions solely in Albanian, and an earnest curatress with a pointer to underline the alleged harm that Catholics, Orthodox and Muslim clerics have done to Albania—and implicitly the rest of the world where they have wrested power. In 1938, runs one graph, there were 144 religious institutions, 48 middle schools, and one health institution in Albania. In 1973, when this oddly touching if dogmatic museum was opened, there were no religious institutions, 307 middle schools, and 371 health institutions. It is hard to tell whether the guide and our interpreter, who kindly softened the rhetoric for the more sensitive old folk among us, really believed all they were saying, for if atheism has one advantage over revealed religions it may be the fact that—for some adherents at least—man-made ideas must occasionally be vulnerable to man-made errors. This unusual slant on history has its own advantages, and indeed reminded me less of Marx and Engels than of pioneer nineteenth-century humanists I had read, such as W.E.H. Lecky, Winwood Reade and J.M. Robertson. But in Western Europe the battle against obscurantist religion is largely won, for even the Vatican is in retreat, and it is only a few diehard Muslim extremist states such as Iran and Libya where religion holds man servile. Politics hold him servile in the Soviet Union, the People's Republic of China, Vietnam, North Korea, and Albania. I left the Muzeu Ateist of Shkodër a chastened atheist, reflecting that intolerance and a closed mind can hold back the progress of unbelievers as well as that of true believers.

Camus has written: 'The interest in rebellion springs from the fact that whole societies have wanted to discard the sacred'. As a totally atheist state since 1967, the Albanian régime has sought to uproot the idea of the sacred, and the worship of the numinous. From a certain human viewpoint, discarding the notion of the superhuman or divine has great advantages. One accepts for the first time complete responsibility for one's actions, and works for the present good of the community, rather than for the potential salvation of one's own soul. But the breadth of sympathy which allows such characters as those of Mother Teresa, Albert Schweitzer, Vinoba Bhave and Gibon Sengai to flourish and affect with love and compassion all around them must not be denied. To mark down as 'class enemies' those who were born to landlords or intellectuals displays stupid, intolerant meanness of spirit. There is no more sense in the 'dictatorship of the proletariat' than there is in any other kind of dictatorship, and it is in any case utterly misleading to think of Albania as governed in any way by its proletariat. The Party of Labour is an elite of Marxist sympathisers and fellow-travellers who decide when and how the Constitution should be changed and who should run the Government and all its apparatus, including education, administration, the law, and the media.

Next morning we saw the elegant Venetian bridge of Mes over the river Kir 5km. north-east of Shkodër, and then took the coach up to the slopes of the Fortress of Rozafat, with magnificent views over the lake and town of Shkodër (the ancient Scodra, which the Italians called Scutari).

Below is the eighteenth-century Leaden Mosque (Xhamië e Plumbit), converted from the Church of St Mark, of course abandoned since 1967. The problem with abolishing religion is the same problem as that of abolishing atheism in an extremist Muslim state (some of which claim to be populated solely by Muslims). One has first to abolish the people. As Brecht's laconic poem *The Solution* puts it:

> After the June the Seventeenth Rebellion
> The Secretary of the Writers' Union
> Had leaflets distributed in the Stalinallee
> To say 'The people had forfeited
> The confidence of the government
> And could win it back
> Only by redoubled labour'.
> Would it not be simpler, then,
> For the government to dissolve the people,
> And elect another?

Comrade Enver was born ten years after Bertolt Brecht (himself a convinced Marxist and propagandist) and seems to have similar views on the functions of a Writers' Union.

This becomes relevant when an old lady dressed in black takes out a cross to show you, and speaks in Italian, the language of the Roman Catholic former colonialists. It is relevant when an old man, openly fingering worry-beads, feels compelled to call out 'La ilahu ill' Allah' when he sees a Muslim tourist, and beams in relief on hearing the comforting reply 'Wa Muhammadun rasul Allah' ('There is no other God but Allah—and Muhammad is His Prophet'). It is relevant when one

Shkodër. From the Fortress of Rozafat.

realises there are five million Albanians in exile with freedom of expression, and only two million living in Albania under a one-party state. A hoarding on the main square in Shkodër reads 'NJE PER TE GJITHE—TE GJITHE PER NJE' ('All for one and one for all'). This is not a suggestion but a command.

High in the Fortress of Rozafat, dominating Shkodër Plain from the south-east, we see west of the town Lake Tarabosh, east of the town Mount Maranaj and the slightly higher Mount Cukali. Just below the fortress the river Buna will run from the lake to the Adriatic Sea, and the medieval town sleeps the sleep of the deserted, surrounded by cypress trees reminiscent of Aquileia. The Fortress of Rozafat was built by the Venetians in the fifteenth century, and strengthened by the Turks when they seized Shkodër a century later, though traces of original Illyrian castle-foundations have been identified. The outer walling, impregnable enough, protects an intermediate wall where one can view the remains of military barracks and a mosque constructed over a ruined church. An inner wall stands guard over a ruined palace used by the Venetian governor, and the water-cisterns essential for survival during siege.

The story of Rozafat told at Shkodër is in fact one of a type so commonly told in the Balkans as to form a genre: the ballad of immurement. Its present-day diffusion throughout south-eastern Europe may indicate a possible Homeric or slightly post-Homeric age, since one example of the ballad may refer to the 3rd-century B.C. foundations of Illyrian Shkodër. Other examples have been found dating from various ages all over the Balkans, and it was widely established by 527–565, when the Greek ballad of the Bridge of Arta must have been composed. Archaeologists have indeed found skeletons immured in foundations by design rather than by accident, so the poem was clearly based on a dread fact.

The ballad's pattern runs as follows. Masons are trying to build a wall (Shkodër) or a bridge (Arta), but whatever they have erected crumbles during the following night. A soothsayer predicts that their work will succeed only if a woman is immured alive. The ballad of Shkodër tells how the young woman, Rozafat, agrees to be immured in the walls to safeguard the whole community from attack but begs that holes be made through which she might still suckle her baby:

'With an eye look upon him,
With a hand caress him,
With a foot cradle him,
With a breast suckle him.'

From this arises the folk superstition that mothers lacking sufficient milk to nourish their children should eat a meal of bread and onions and then anoint their nipples with limey water found condensed on the fortress walls. With its white tinge, this water is supposed to derive from the entombed mother's breast.

An Albanian ballad from Dukagjin sung during the various Ottoman incursions quotes the dying words of a woman immured to secure the fortress:

'And never, my son, desert it;
Though the Turk come and seize it,
Though the wilderness overrun it,
Though the lightning split and smash it'.

Eventually, masons were persuaded to have more confidence in their own work, and a live chicken or small animal replaced human sacrifice (reminding one of Abraham, Isaac, and the ram in the thicket). Later still, and we are speaking of our own century now, a wooden image of a woman sufficed—for a bridge over the river Osum at Berat.

Shkodër was the capital of the Ardian tribe of Illyrians from the 3rd century B.C., its river Buna (classical Barbana) being navigable from the city to the sea. The Romans made it a key station on their road north from Dyrrachium, and the Byzantines also found it worth their while to control the city, though in the age of mediaeval feudalism local chieftains exercised increasing power, shifting alliances at home and abroad. The great Venetian merchants seized Shkodër, which they named Scutari (for good Venetian reasons) in 1396 and held on until the furious onslaught of the Ottomans in the fifteenth century. Suleiman Pasha attacked in 1473, losing 14,000 men from a force of 80,000, and retired mortified. Five years later Mehmet Pasha returned with an estimated 250,000 men and, despite losing up to 30,000, finally achieved victory by surrender of the Fortress in January 1479. The besiegers stood aghast when they saw how pitifully few were the defenders—the story is told by Marino Barlezio in *De obsidione Scodrensis* (Venice, 1505), a work predating by five years the completed publication of his chronicle of Skënderbeg, *Historia de vita et gestis Skanderbegi epirotarum principis*. The defence of Scutari is the subject of a heroic painting by one of Paolo Veronese's school in the Sala del Maggior Consiglio, in the Venetian Ducal Palace. Painted after the fire of 1577, and already finished by 1585, the painting is depressingly rhetorical, and so far below Veronese's best as to be scarcely worth a glance, were it not for one's fortuitous interest in the theme, which the school of Veronese could hardly have known at first hand.

With the decadence of Ottoman administration, Shkodër became a hereditary *pashalik* under the control of the Bushatli family, thriving especially under the strong hand of Kara Mahmut Bushatli (1775–1831). Weapons, furs and clothes were manufactured here, and he united the north by subduing the pirates of Ulcinj (now in Montenegro, Yugoslavia).

Shkodër was besieged under Hussein Riza Bey by the Serbs and Montenegrins from 25 October 1912 to 23 April 1913. It was on 29 July 1913 that the Ambassadors' Conference in London recognised Albania's independence, giving it more or less the boundaries it possesses today, and pronounced it a 'Sovereign hereditary principality, whose neutrality was guaranteed by the Great Powers'. The borders enclosed about 28,000 square kilometres, with a population then approaching 800,000. Kosova, a largely Albanian area, was cut off and enclosed with Serbia. (This caused a problem still very much with us as the University of Prishtina (Yugoslavia) remains closed following student demonstrations alleging anti-Albanian measures by the Government.) Cameria was cut off and enclosed within Greece.

The ambitious Esat Pasha Toptani (from Central Albania) had caused the Turkish commander of Shkodër (Hussein Riza) to be murdered and took charge himself at the end of April 1913, then surrendered the city to Montenegro, in exchange for a promise that he would become prince or king of Albania in the future. He then left Shkodër in the hands of the

Montenegrins and moved south, occupying with his army both Tirana and Durrës, in opposition to the Albanian National Assembly movement which had been gaining momentum under Ismail Qemal since 28 November 1912. Shkodër was occupied by an international naval force under Admiral Sir Cecil Burney until 1914. The Serbs took the town on 27 June 1915, followed by the Austrians (23 January 1916), and the Italians and French (November 1918 to March 1920). The Regency was set up in 1920, with four regents (two Muslims, one Orthodox and one Roman Catholic) and Albania was recognised by the Great Powers on 9 November 1921, and joined the League of Nations on 17 December 1921. Now there arose the fundamental conflict between Ahmet Zogu, son of a Muslim tribal chief of the Mat zone and at the age of twenty-six Minister of the Interior in Delvina's 1920 administration, and Fan Noli, nicknamed 'the Red Bishop', who led what has become known subsequently as the 'bourgeois democratic revolution of June 1924'. Bishop Noli, an Albanian American from Harvard, put forward proposals which would sweep away apathy and feudalism and introduce civil liberties, agrarian reform, the rule of law, compulsory education, and judicial, fiscal and administrative reforms. Such revolutionary ideas found numerous antagonists, so that when Ahmet Zogu, invading from Yugoslavia, entered Tirana on 14 December 1924, he encountered little resistance.

In January 1925 Zogu convened the National Assembly which proclaimed the Albanian Republic, Zogu to serve as regent for seven years from 1 February. With the steady improvement in relations between Mussolini and Zogu, culminating in the 1927 defence pact against the alleged Franco-Yugoslav treaty, Zogu felt strong enough to instal himself as King Zog I by unanimous decree of 1 September 1928. The Italians invaded on Good Friday 1939, and Germans occupied Albania from 11 September 1943 to 29 November 1944. On 17 November 1944 Tirana was free from its last invaders, and on 29 November Shkodër was liberated.

Until September 1948 the Yugoslavs attempted to wield power with the Albanians. From September 1948 to November 1960 the Russians wooed Comrade Enver with economic and technical assistance. Between 1961 and 1977 China pursued a similar line of friendship with assistance. In each case, Albania ultimately believed its independence was threatened, and rightly or wrongly construed economic aid as bribery intended to subvert national and political independence. Albania sincerely believes it is the only country pursuing the true and original Marxist-Leninist ideology (though Marxism and Leninism are themselves hardly synonymous), and takes the Stalinist period of Soviet history as a

Shkodër. Reception for
delegates returning from
the Trades Union Congress,
1982.

model, when expressed in purely Albanian terms. Like all one-party
states, it tends to love vociferously and hate vociferously, believing that
'those who are not for us must be against us'. Yet that may not be true.

All attempts to enforce uniformity of political, economic or religious
beliefs will stifle a nation's life-blood as assuredly as a tourniquet twisted
tight on a patient's arm. Society will continue to require constant diversi-
fication in life-styles and financial investment as the population increases
and communications proliferate. A society like Albania which fails to
generate risk wealth is making no contribution to the future of the world,
and is in danger of becoming a curiosity—a backwater—a museum of
past agricultural and industrial techniques. The peculiar Albanian
interpretation of Marxism-Leninism through the distorting prisms of
Stalinism and Maoism has left Albania out of joint with the times: even
Stalin would not behave Stalinistically if he were alive and powerful
today. Economics should not rule a nation's life: respect for civil liberties
balanced with the rule of constitutional law should. Engels himself
ridiculed those who saw economics as pivotal to Communism.
'According to the materialist view of history', he said, 'production and
reproduction of real life are, *in the last instance*, the determining factor in
history. Neither Marx nor I have asserted more than that. If anyone
twists this into a claim that the economic factor is the *only* determinant,
he transforms our statement into a meaningless, abstract, absurd phrase.'

Scientific evidence from the amoeba to the hominid tends to the
conclusion that evolution in all fields has been from the simple to the

complex, from the general to the particular. In classifying flora, for example, we began with a few genera and have arrived at hundreds of thousands of species, and the tendency continues to work in this way. In human society, the earliest anthropoids were relatively undifferentiated as regards racial type, physical features, and needs, whereas now we have such a multiplicity of individual types and such fragmentation in society that complex nations like the U.S.A. and India are constantly threatened by the conflicting demands of their inhabitants. The easiest political solution to such a conflict of interests is for a dictator to impose his will on the rest of society, not only 'making the trains run on time' but also eliminating by force those ideas which struggle with his own for survival. Hitler was of this type, and so was Stalin. The Chinese Cultural Revolution exemplified the phenomenon, as did the extermination campaign of Pol Pot against Khmer intellectuals, and Somoza's against the intellectuals of Nicaragua.

But the easiest political solution is not necessarily the best. While opponents of American capitalism might argue that it has failed because it is no longer safe to walk in East Los Angeles, on the positive side it can be shown that social assistance makes life tolerable for millions who would have starved a century ago. If it is safe for us to walk alone at night along the streets of Albania, it might also be argued that a population held in check by fear of the authorities can have no effective reply if the authorities themselves act lawlessly.

2
Lezhë and Durrës

We left Shkodër by the southern route that runs beside the river Drin, and through villages with exotic names: Bërdicë, Bushat, Barbullush, Kakarriq, Balldren... Defensive concrete bunkers gaze with unblinking eye-slits as we overtake bullock-carts, and parp unwary urchins out of the roadway. Mulberries, vines, and vegetables are grown in this region, and the swamps of Kakarriq, once notorious, have been replaced by fertile fields. The Drin has caused disastrous flooding over the centuries, but it is now tamed for irrigation.

One-and-a-half kilometres before entering Lezhë the road forks right to Shëngjin, a small port known in antiquity as Nymphaeum, and more recently as San Giovanni di Medua ('Shën' means 'Saint' and 'Gjin' is 'John'). Shëngjin, seven kilometres from Lezhë, has a fine sandy beach but no hotel: one uses that at Ishull, in Lezhë.

Lezhë

Illyrian and classical Lissus was situated on Mount Ascension (Mal e Shelbumit), a bare hill above Lezhë which still possesses its ruined Illyrian ramparts overshadowing the walls erected under the hegemony of Dionysius of Syracuse (385 B.C.). But Dionysius, having dreamt of conquering the Adriatic from Sicily, found Lissus soon overrun by Ardian Illyrians, who took power until the Romans under Julius Caesar conquered the city and rebuilt it after his battle in 48 B.C. From 1391 to 1449 it was held by Serbs, then by the Dukagjin feudal chieftains, passing to the Venetians in 1493 and to the Turks in 1498. Gjergj Kastrioti Skënderbeg convened the Albanian League here in March 1444, and after many heady victories it was here too that the national hero died on 17 January 1468. To mark the quincentenary of his death, in 1968, the ruined Franciscan church of Shën Koll (St Nicholas), which had been converted into a mosque during the Ottoman occupation, was declared a national monument. It is the burial-place of Skënderbeg, whose feats have been the subjects of many epics and novels such as Naim Frashëri's *Istori e Skënderbeut*, a long poem in folk-ballad metre popular among

Lezhë. Hunting Lodge.

◁ Lezhë. Skënderbeg's Tomb.

all literate Albanians since the last decade of the nineteenth century, and Ismail Kadare's novel *Kështjella* (1970), translated into English as *The Castle* (1974).

Whether you come to Lezhë for lunch or to spend the night, it would be impossible to conceive a more tranquil spot. By a riverbank, under shady trees, with lizards and dragonflies darting unexpectedly in front of you, you find a rickety wooden bridge that leads into a copse. Frogs make their customary din; the wind soughs in the branches overhead, and the sun glitters in the waters. The insects I knew as waterboatmen as a boy skid upstream on the surface of the river like kids running up a down escalator. Fig-trees bear within them latent fruit. Tortoises amble under acacias.

And then lunch is called: we enter the single-storey hotel, shutters drawn against insects, and then it dawns on me, fool that I am! This is Mussolini's hunting lodge! The opulent leather chairs, the open fireplace for winter wood-burning, the timbered ceiling and carefully-planned rusticity of the décor: all combined to help il Duce and his men relax after a morning's shooting in the marshes. I turned up a paragraph in Brunialti and Grande's *Il Mediterraneo* (1927) which gives a clue to the preoccupations of the Italians twelve years before they took control.

Referring to Albania, Stefano Grande observes: "There are important exports of sardines and anchovies, while trout and sturgeon are found in the rivers. Deer, hare, boar, chamois, and marsh-birds could all become significant game, but hunting at present attracts only rich travellers, who consider this country almost as if it were Africa, carrying out profitable hunts."

As soon as Hitler occupied Czechoslovakia, Mussolini resolved himself in the direction 'of a blow in Albania'. Vittorio Emanuele advised against risking a war 'to grab four rocks', but on 28 March 1939 il Duce was made delirious with joy at the news of Franco's victory for Fascism in Madrid; at dawn ten days later Italian troops landed in Albania and took the country with little opposition.

Suddenly we are transported in time more than forty years: the little weekend lodge at Lezhë, tucked away from the main road in idyllic surroundings, represents a world quite tamed, where man is master over the birds of the air and the beasts of the field. It is easy to see why tourism too is tamed, with only three hundred visitors a year from Britain and the Commonwealth, and roughly the same numbers from other hard-currency nations. Comrade Enver has contradicted the general tendency to mass tourism which has ruined so much of Spain, Italy and Greece, for example, in the following words: "Why should we turn our land into an inn with doors flung open to pigs and sows, to boys and girls with pants on or no pants at all? Why should we let the long-haired hippies supplant with their wild orgies the graceful dances of our people?" (*The Listener*, 22 April 1982). These are good and pertinent questions, and can be related to the absence of litter and tipping (equally obnoxious to capitalist Iceland and communist China, however), and to the generally unspoilt nature of the countryside. If one is tempted to ask why Albanian youngsters should not be allowed to listen to pop music, rock, funk, punk and all the other commercially-manipulated fashions of Western democracies—and indeed of Hungary or Yugoslavia—then one might also be tempted to ask what positive benefit such fads and crazes bring the youngsters who already possess them.

Lezhë at least is Arcadia for dusty travellers. After a leisurely amble through the grounds of the hunting lodge we sat down to fresh soup made from locally-grown vegetables, prawns and salad, beef and potatoes, and peaches, the whole washed down with red or white wine according to taste, or mineral water at 2 leks (17 pence) for a large bottle. Some visitors later reported having drunk the local water throughout Albania, and suffering no ill-effects, but this is not generally advised.

At length we clambered contentedly back on the coach and headed on to the dusty high road to Tirana, passing the village of Zejmen and the river Mat before entering the new town of Laç. Like so much of the coastal plain, the zone around Laç was a malarial swamp until it was cleared a generation ago: rice and reeds now flourish, and three factories have been built (for glass, copper-smelting, and super-phosphates), attracting workers from all over Albania.

Beyond Laç the growing town of Mamurras is predominantly agricultural: I was astonished to see corn growing between fruit trees. Here and farther south is the huge state farm named for Skënderbeg, and ten minutes later we arrived at the cross-roads of Fushë-Krujë, the name meaning Krujë-in-the-Plain. Strategically vital, Fushë-Krujë is 7km. north-east of Tirana, and 40km. north-west of Durrës. The ubiquitous bunkers in the countryside illustrate the constant state of alertness that the Albanian leadership inculcates into the citizens: every man is reputed to sleep with a loaded rifle at the ready, and great red banners in the towns urge UNITET, GATISHMËRI, VIGJILENCË (Unity, Readiness, Vigilance).

Community, Identity, and Stability might be the motto of contemporary Albania: but then, it is also the motto of the World State in Aldous Huxley's *Brave new world*. 'It would be sheer cruelty to afflict them with excessive leisure,' says Mustapha Mond in *Brave new world*. 'It's the same with agriculture. We could synthesize every morsel of food, if we wanted to. But we don't. We prefer to keep a third of the population on the land. For their own sakes—because it takes *longer* to get food out of the land than out of a factory. Besides, we have our stability to think of. We don't want to change. Every change is a menace to stability.'

Six kilometres south of Fushë-Krujë, high on a hill, we see the regional observation post, used by Albanians for centuries to warn Krujë of the presence of incoming troops from the West. Albanians have known subjugation for so many centuries—indeed the modern boundaries are only seven decades old—that independence is still a word to stir the heart of the man-in-the-street, and the pen of the writer.

As the bus bumped along the poor highway which is Albania's nearest equivalent to a motorway, we pondered the vulnerability of this sliver of territory defended by 2½ million people. The borders with Yugoslavia (465km.) and Greece (228km.) are wide open to attack by any threatening army, while the long coastline has only four defensive ports: the tiny Shëngjin in the north, Durrës in the centre, the natural harbour of Vlorë in the south, and Sarandë in the far south. Of these, Vlorë if captured would lead to a stranglehold on the oilfields, but to capture the capital, the broadcasting stations and the administration, one would need first to be master of Durrës.

25

Durrës

Durrës, with a population of about sixty thousand, is—with Shkodër—the second largest city of Albania. The visitor keen to stay on the beach will like Durrës better than anywhere else in the country, for the rocky coast near Sarandë is really only for strong sea-swimmers: there is hardly any sand and only one hotel.

Dusty Tirana is only 42km. to the east, but it seems a world away from the glittering golden sand and welcoming waters of the beaches south of Durrës. A disadvantage of these beach hotels lies in the fact of their distance from Durrës city. Regent Holidays state that foreigners may not use the buses or trains (though at least two of my acquaintances used the local bus from Durrës, flat fare of 30 qindarkas), so that in the heat of the day the two miles back may dissuade the less adventurous from exploring on their own. But if you saunter slowly, and keep your eyes open, the walk can be very pleasant, shaded as it is by avenues most of the way. You follow the curve of the bay from Durrës centre, keeping the railway line on your right until one track suddenly bends inland towards Tirana.

Durrës rather than Tirana is the rail capital of Albania. Until the national railway network was inaugurated in 1946, there were only two railway lines: a 31km. Decauville track taking bitumen from the mine at Selenicë 31km. to Skele, the port 3km. south of Vlorë, with extensions; and a much shorter line between Shkozët and Lekaj, south of Durrës,

Train.

which was in military use just before World War I. Now trains run twice a day between Shkodër and Durrës via Lezhë and Laç; six times a day between Tirana and Durrës; twice a day from Durrës to Elbasan (one extending to Pogradec); and twice a day from Durrës to Fier (one extending to Ballsh). A line is under construction to link Fier with Vlorë. Apart from steam shunting at Durrës, all trains run on diesel. Photography in this area is of course banned.

The pioneer camp at Durrës can accommodate 1,350 children between the ages of 10 and 14 divided into three units each of 450 children, each of which is further subdivided into fifteen sub-units of thirty children. They prepare and cook their own meals, and organise their own programmes, which include political discussions and debates, swimming, singing, and games.

You can gain a fair idea of Albania-on-holiday from the workers' chalets, beach villas, and then the Albturist hotels (first-class Adriatiku and second-class Durrësi, Butrinti and Apollonia, with a total of 1500 beds).

There is no open affection between couples, for that is considered shameful. Women on the beaches are outnumbered about one to eight by menfolk.

I was hectored by a grizzled old man sitting on the grass surrounded by bottles of beer, most of them empty: he inveighed in a muddled way against Fascist Poles and Germans, doubtless taking me for one or (as he was tipsy) possibly both.

Oleanders were in brilliant bloom on that sunny June day. Poplars waved sedately, serenely, casting elegant and all-encompassing shade on the patched-up road. I played soccer barefoot on the beach with three lads in search of a fourth, then invited them to a lemonade or beer by a cabin, watching the bullock-carts creak by.

'A jeni martuar?' queried my partner. (Are you married?) 'Po, unë kam dy vajza' (Yes, I have two daughters). They came from Tirana, and were secondary-school pupils. One of them began to tell me of his parents, but the other two quickly shut him up and, after politely shaking my hand and thanking me for the drinks, the trio made off guiltily. Then I saw a soldier emerge from behind a tree, and realised why the foreigner had been left by himself. We had also been steadfastly observed by a little girl so sombre that she looked as if she had been given her first doll only two weeks before being expected to dress and undress a baby brother and is still brooding, years later, on being cheated of her childhood.

At a little kiosk marked LIBRARI I purchased an exercise-book for notes, the daily newspaper *Zëri i Popullit* (*Voice of the People*), and

Comrade Enver Hoxha's *Reflections on China* (1962–1977). Over lunch, I started to read the 1593-page *Reflections*, which are extracts from Comrade Enver's political diary. I recalled as I was reading that incredible day—it was actually 16 November 1960 and is commemorated by a painting in the National Museum—when Enver Hoxha had stood up in the Moscow conference of 81 communist parties, and denounced the Khrushchev line, which favoured Tito and finally repudiated Stalin. He moved so close to the Maoist line that the Chinese, then isolated in world opinion, felt that Albania could become a useful European outpost, and began to cultivate Comrade Enver. Year by year the Chinese came closer to Albania, and the Fourth Five-Year Plan (1966–1970) was over-fulfilled, thanks partly to cautious targets and partly to Chinese aid. The Fifth Five-Year Plan (1971–1975) was also successful in some sectors, but failed in others, the failures being attributed to 'sabotage' by the Chinese. Whatever the truth of these allegations, such as that an oil-refinery was left half-completed, and spare parts failed to arrive, the fact is that due to its allies and its own efforts Albania has become self-sufficient in electricity and now exports hydro-electric power to Yugoslavia from the power station on the Drin (formerly named for Mao Tse-tung) near Shkodër.

Industrial growth has been gravely hampered by a constitutional provision preventing the negotiation of foreign loans. In 1979 Albania was the world's third largest exporter of chrome, and in 1981 it had become the second. Oil production declined from 2.5 million tonnes in the mid-1970s to 1.5 million tonnes in 1980, a figure 20% below the level targeted. The output of high-grade steel from the Mao Tse-tung Steel Factory (now the Steel of the Party Combine) at Elbasan stopped for some time after the break with China because of the absence of skilled labour, but technicians are being sent to the West for training and some production has resumed.

The 1971–5 Plan showed an annual average growth in industrial production of 8.7%, but this fell to a disappointing 6.2% in the 1976–80 Plan, probably due to the absence of pay incentives for increased productivity. Experience in the People's Republic of China has shown that, if the workers are given *some* incentive, such as a chance to keep livestock or tend their own vegetable patch, enthusiasm waxes at work as well as at home: in Albania too it might be that the faceless uniformity of farm and factory, with virtually no privacy or opportunities for creative individuality, stamps out among many the will to work. The Albanians in times gone by were fiercely individualistic, brave, warlike. Hospitable to neutral strangers, they were unforgiving, unforgettingly ruthless enemies. Self-reliance is an Albanian trait which the Party of

Labour has seized on: but its most telling facet is in private enterprise, which has been virtually eliminated. The Party of Labour recognises the discrepancy between theory and practice by planning an average annual increase in industrial output over the 1981–5 Plan period of 6.0–6.3% as against a planned labour productivity of only 2.5–2.8% a year. (The output figures in the 1971–5 Plan period showed an annual increase of 8.7%, as a comparative indicator). Real income per head is not likely to rise by more than 2% a year. During the 1976–80 Plan period, national income was targeted to rise by 38–40% over the previous period: the rise was in fact only 25.2%.

After a breakfast next day of omelette, rough but nutritious greyish bread, butter and jam, with tea and sugar but no milk, we were driven in our Albturist coach to the Archaeological and Ethnographical Museum of Durrës, facing the sea. Entrance is free, as it is everywhere else in Albania, to all archaeological sites and museums. On the negative side, you will never find any postcards, guidebooks, or leaflets on sale, and the captions are invariably only in Albanian, so it becomes quite important to remember for instance that 'Shekulli V para erës sonë' means 'Fifth century before our era' (thus expressed because 'Before Christ' would invoke a name not to be mentioned in Albania).

Durrës. Funerary stele in the
Archaeological Museum.

The museum is in a two-storey building with a basement, but only the ground-floor is open to visitors, together with the garden. Room 1 is distinguished by an Illyrian helmet, a few Illyrian inscriptions, and a 6th-century *krater* from the necropolis. Room 2 displays some fine Apulian red-figure vases, and some sculptured heads without adequate captions. One glimpses in frustration through a barred window a basement stacked with sherds and funerary urns packed in wooden Chinese boxes, and therefore obviously untouched for years. The courtyard reveals an ill-assorted jumble of lead pipes, a few sculptures vandalised by time, amphorae for storing wine, water and olive oil, an Osmanli gravestone, and cannonballs stacked neatly by one side of a reconstructed forum. If only the Durrës Museum were to benefit from some of the museological skills shown in the new Ethnographical Museum in Tirana, for example! But the Albanian Government has chosen for its priorities agriculture and industry, and who should criticise these priorities? I suppose that one's disappointment in Durrës Museum stems from the fact that the city's history is profoundly interesting, yet little emerges from a visit to the institution nominally set aside to provoke and stimulate such interest.

Dyrrhachion (the port) and Epidamnos (the defended city) were originally founded from Corinth and Corfu in the late seventh century B.C., and quickly developed into a major entrepôt for ships plying between Greece and Italy, since after the harbour of Vlorë (the classical Avlon), its harbour was the finest on the eastern Adriatic coast. Gradually the name Epidamnos fell into disuse, and coins minted there bear the name Dyrrhachion. When the city took issue with Corfu, Athens took the part of Corfu while Corinth sent aid to Dyrrhachion in 435 B.C., thus indirectly offering a pretext for the Peloponnesian War (432–404 B.C.) so brilliantly narrated by Thucydides and Xenophon. The native Illyrians (from whom at least some modern Albanian mountain-dwellers trace their ancestry) had constantly harried the Greek colonists, but under Glaukias they finally took the city in 232, and three years later proclaimed an alliance as a free city with Rome against their former rulers, at the same time as Apollonia.

Durrës is the western terminus of the Roman Via Egnatia to Thessaloniki and Constantinople, studied by O'Sullivan in *The Egnatian Way* (1972). If you want to follow the Via Egnatia from Durrës, simply take the road to Elbasan and Prrenjas, via Kavajë, Rrogozhinë (Mutatio Clodiana), Trajectus, Candavia, Tabernas, and Qukës (Claudanon). If you choose to take your own car, you can take a car ferry from Bari, fifty miles north of Brindisi, in eight hours to Bar (Yugoslavia), then through Montenegro to Struga in Macedonia, joining the Egnatian Way as it emerges from Albania, and continuing from Ohrid to Bitota (Heracleia), Bistrica, Florina (Melitonus) and Vevi (Mutatio Grande).

All eyes in the ancient world were anxiously cast on Illyria during the first of the Civil Wars, in 49 B.C. Pompey controlled Dyrrachium, but after seven months of marching, attack, and counter-attack, the forces of Caesar were totally victorious at Pharsalia, not far from Volos. The story, which is quite absorbing, can best be assimilated in Robert Graves' version from Lucan's *Pharsalia*. We know of seventy Christian families in Dyrrachium in 58 A.D., under the care of a bishop; in 449 the town was elevated to an archiepiscopate, and the Byzantine Emperor Anastasios I (491–518) took good care to defend his vitally strategic port and home town with three circuits of walls after an invading force of Goths had besieged in 481.

Anna Comnena's *Alexiad* (translated by E.R.A. Sewter, 1969) is our best source for the Norman invasion of 1081–3 from Apulia under Robert Guiscard. Anna married Nicephorus Bryennius, son of Alexios Comnenus' enemy of the same name.

Anna, daughter of Alexios I Comnenos (1081–1181) has left us an enthralling account of contemporary Dyrrachium and the attacks on the city of Bohemond, son of Robert Guiscard, who tried battering-rams against the walls, tunnelling underneath the walls, and finally (having begun it before the other devices), a wooden tower to conquer from above the walls. 'First, however,' writes Anna, 'I must briefly explain the plan of Dyrrachium. Its wall is interrupted by towers which all round the city rise to a height of eleven feet above it. A spiral staircase leads to the top of the towers and they are strengthened by battlements. The walls are of considerable thickness, so wide indeed that more than four horsemen can ride abreast in safety... A wooden tower, built to a considerable height on a four-sided base, was so high that the city towers were overtopped by at least five cubits, so that the enemy ramparts might be overrun when the tower's drawbridges were lowered... The tower was indeed a terrible sight, but it was even more terrible in motion, for its base was raised on rollers by soldiers who jacked it up on levers. Since the cause of the motion was invisible, it seemed self-propelled and the defenders were amazed. It had been covered from top to bottom and on all four sides for good defence, but slits had been made on every storey from which besiegers could fire showers of arrows, and the top was filled by the leading swordsmen of Bohemond's army.

Yet even against this monster Alexios had devised ingenious defence. After seeing how the invaders' tower had been made, and how high it was, the defenders set up a scaffolding on a square base, with floors erected at intervals up the four-pole scaffolding to a height one cubit above the invaders' tower, and roofed. Liquid fire was then carried up to the roof and hurled over the wall, but the jets of fire barely reached the tower, so they filled the space between the tower and the scaffolding with combustible material, poured huge quantities of oil on it, and set it alight with torches, quickly escaping from the open-sided scaffolding to safety. The invaders trapped inside the tower were quickly incinerated, and those on the highest platform leapt to the ground, dying or breaking limbs (at best). Thus did Alexios I Comnenos foil the siege of Bohemond.'

If Anna admired her father's achievements, she never underestimated the brilliance of Bryennius as a bold adventurer and wily tactician. Withdrawing in 1109, the Normans retook Dyrrachium briefly under William of Sicily in 1185, but it was captured by the Crusaders, who made it over to Venice in 1203. Falling successively to the Emperor Theodorus (1205), to Manfred of Sicily (1258), to Charles of Anjou (1272), the Franks of Achaia, and the Serbs, the city was retaken by the Venetians in 1392 and strengthened with new fortifications. The Ottoman Turks, who took Durrës in 1501, let it droop and slumber through more than four centuries, so that reports in 1880 could refer to this former capital of Illyria as 'a small village'. In 1916 its population was barely six hundred, when the Austrians made it a submarine base. Durrës was the headquarters of the provisional government of Albania from Christmas Day 1918 to 27 March 1920.

Durrës today is a place very different from the old Turkish village of narrow streets and jealously-high walls, restricting the pedestrian's view of the interiors of homes and gardens. Wide tree-lined boulevards necklace the harbour, with its merchant ships and massive cranes. If Tirana is the Cosenza of Albania, then Durrës is its Brindisi, although the analogy cannot be pushed too far.

One is shown the Roman amphitheatre, discovered in 1660 to be submerged below a curiously-shaped hill. Seventy houses were eventually demolished, to reveal a seated ellipse 120 metres at its greatest length. The laconic pace of excavation continues, so that even today one is assured that there are some houses still to be removed before the 'final' phase of excavations can begin. The amphitheatre seems to have been cut out of the hill above the port in the 2nd century A.D. ('of our era', I should say, to avoid wounding Albanian sensibility) to accommodate about 20,000 spectators. It was abandoned in the Middle Ages, and a Byzantine church and associated cemetery were allowed to sully Carnival with Lent. Parts of the galleries, staircases, and arena may be visited, and one shivers in anticipation in the suddenly dark cave where the lions, tigers and other beasts were kept until their turn should come.

Durrës. Roman amphitheatre.

As you emerge, Byzantine walls rear up outside the enclosed amphitheatre to exemplify the nature of palimpsest.

Since ancient Dyrrachium lies below modern Durrës, the authorities have taken the unusual step of declaring the whole city a national archaeological site, so that no digging can take place without prior authorisation. This policy can be justified by taking the example of the Woman's Head mosaic, discovered in the residential quarter of the city and published in Skënder Anamali and Stilian Adhami's *Mozaikë të Shqipërisë* (Tirana, 1974). Of the fourth-century A.D., it consists of a dark pebble background with contrasting flesh-coloured pebbles for the face, expressive lips but rather lifeless eyes, the best and most imaginative aspect of the design being the brilliant floral ornamentation around the head: this may indeed be the goddess Flora, though there is no external corroboration of internal evidence.

The Roman baths complex of Durrës was uncovered as recently as 1962, when the Palace of Culture was being erected, within it the Alexandre Moïsiu Theatre, named for the city's finest actor, who rose to international celebrity. The hypocaust has been exposed, and we can admire the symmetrical chessboard paving and the bathing-pool 7m. long by 5.3m. wide.

Durrës is primarily an industrial district, two thirds of its total production being industrial and one third agricultural, but we were taken

33

to a State Agricultural Enterprise near Durrës called 8 Nandori 1941 (8 November 1941) after the date of the formation of the Communist Party (now the 'Party of Labour') of Albania. Little girls waving wooden rifles by the side of the road wore red pioneer scarves round their necks. Shady avenues are welcome, since almost everyone has to walk: there are no private cars or motor-cycles, so it is the height of ambition to own a bicycle. Formerly, bicycles were imported from China, but now there is a factory in Tirana to produce bikes for men, women and children, even if demand will probably outstrip supply for many years to come.

The state farm began in 1944 with 900 hectares and one small imported tractor. Now it has a hundred Albanian-made tractors to work 4,500 hectares. Marshes have been drained, barren hillsides cleared, and the huge farm complex houses 12,000 inhabitants, 4,500 of them state workers. The farm exports potatoes, tomatoes, water-melons and grapes to such countries as West Germany, Austria and Finland; it runs local dairy shops for workers, and sells to state enterprises in Durrës and Tirana. The farm specialises in wheat, vegetables and dairy produce in nine production sections and three auxiliary sections. Workers are paid an average of 600 leks per month (roughly £50 or US$90) for 6 eight-hour days a week. It is claimed that trade unions experience no difficulty with strikes, disputes, or wage-claims that cannot be resolved by discussion and persuasion, and indeed for whatever reason there is no record of strike action anywhere in Albania since the dawn of the Communist age. The farm not only runs its own clinics and schools, but also offers evening classes for adults and entertainment in its own Palace of Culture, making it possible for the average worker not to move from the farm throughout his life. A married woman is allowed leave for six months after the birth of a child, and rest on a wage of 80% of her current income. The apparently abysmal level of pay can be explained partly by the facts that there is no personal income tax, there is no envy of highly-paid workers since nobody earns more than twice the minimum wage, that prices are fixed throughout the country by the state, that rents are low (about 45 leks for a two-room flat in Tirana and less out here), and that most consumer goods are just not available even if one could afford to buy them.

I was mystified to find that most families could afford a television set (4,500 leks), equivalent to about nine months' salary, and nearly everyone had access to a radio (1,000 leks in the shops). Repair-shops for all kinds of electrical and mechanical goods are to be found on every street, for Albanians carry thrift to its logical conclusion in this as in matters of clothing and entertainment. Olive oil and flour were rationed during my visit, but other shortages could be ascribed either to uncoordinated imports and local production, or to unavailability of hard currency. Albania's development is slow partly because of a laudable stubbornness in self-reliance. It may be cheaper for the leadership to get people to mend old machines (it certainly wastes time and impedes the economic development of the country). It also saves hard currency and leads to a possibly admirable facet of patriotism—the sentimental unity that in another context gives us *The Eton Boating Song* ('We'll all pull toGETHAH!') or cohesion to a national football team drawn from eleven different clubs.

The Hotel Adriatiku has a sun terrace spread with pink oleanders, easy access to the public beach and the 24-hour post office next door, a tennis court, a 'tavern' for dancing at night, a bookshop, and a private bathroom with shower in each of its 67 rooms. On fine summer nights foreign guests in Durrës are offered open-air Albanian films with English sub-titles, usually on the roof of the Hotel Durrësi. When the weather is chillier, films are arranged in a room on the ground floor of the Hotel Adriatiku. On our way from the restaurant we passed posters and displays in the foyer showing seven photographs of Shoku Enver 'From One Party Congress to Another'. STEEL-LIKE UNITY ran one slogan above pictures of agriculture and industry: GRANDIOUS BALANCE-SHEET. GLORIOUS PROSPECT. We emerged into the splendour of an Adriatic sunset, and strolled across the terrace past the exhortation in English to sinful Western bathers: 'Obligatory consume! Undressing forbidden! No clothes on tables or chairs! In case of undressing and shower need, apply to the reception according to the regulation!'

The film, which ran from 8 p.m. to 9.50, was *The Girls with Red Ribbons*. Set about 1940, during the Italian occupation, it shows a girls' school run by the Italians, with some collaborating teachers. Family life is dominated by heroes who plan to demonstrate against the Fascists during a visit to Tirana by the Minister Paolo Ferrara. Some girls wear red ribbons as a mark of communist defiance, and unite against a girl who informs her teachers and the headmaster about the activities of the ringleaders. The film ends with the tragic death of the heroine by firing squad after having taken part in the demonstration, but the future is rosy as her example is taken up like a flag by those who loved her.

We no longer make simplistic films like this in the West, so we can only compare *The Girls with Red Ribbons* with Stalinist films from the Soviet Union, and with the output from China during the Cultural Revolution. The motive for making films is exclusively nationalistic: no 'realism' is attempted, but sentimentality and cardboard cut-out 'good' and 'bad' characters take the place of real personalities. The camera-work is naive, and the sound blurred.

All other films emerging from the state-owned industry are equally two-dimensional, offering neither artistic nor intellectual challenge to the audience, but emphasising only that same ideology in the evening which they have read in the morning paper and practised at work all day. Here are a few typical scenarios of recent films.

Vladimir Prifti's *The Road of Letters* and Muharem Fejzo's *The School*, both set in the nineteenth century, deal with efforts to spread education and literature in Albanian through schools and printing presses, despite the efforts of the Turkish rulers to suppress the language. The line is that the Turks wished to impose Islam and Turkish, while the Orthodox and Roman Catholic priests tried to indoctrinate the people with Christianity, Greek, Latin and Italian.

Concert in the Year 1936, directed by Saimir Kumbaro, deals with the life of Tefta Koço, a French-trained singer who returns to King Zog's Albania to give concert-tours with a pianist. When they arrive in a provincial town, they are treated with deference by the Chief of Police until he discovers that they are artistes. The Sub-Prefect protects them from suspicion but he too recoils in horror when he realises that they plan to include a song in defence of democracy. The authorities now try to ban the concert, but the townspeople threaten them with civil disobedience and force them to attend the concert, which is then turned into a demonstration against the régime. One can only make a comparison with the current ban on touring companies by foreigners in Albania. When the Secretary of the Albanian Society offered a British Film Festival to the Albanians, he was allowed to provide a one-day selection ranging from a 1905 classic about a dog to documentaries on British problems of race and industry.

In the White Forests There is Life, directed by Rikard Llarja, shows the benign influence of hard-working lumberjacks and geologists on a self-centred intellectual from Tirana, isolated by snow in the remote highlands of Albania. The Party of Labour requires all bureaucrats, intellectuals and army officers to spend a month each year on 'productive labour' either in agriculture or industry. The theory is that intellectuals should not pass their critical and analytical views (if any) to the working classes, but that the working classes should 'reform' by their example of uncontaminated ideology and hard manual labour the innate tendencies of the manager to make decisions based on efficiency and of the intellectual to make decisions based on abstract principles and pragmatic considerations. A decision in Albania must be based solely on ideological grounds: if it conforms to Marxist-Leninist thought with a Stalinist tinge, it is correct; if not, it is incorrect. Moreover, the hero of *In the White Forests There is Life* must be reformed by the end of the film, since films in Albania must be optimistic rather than realistic: single-minded rather than multi-faceted.

One day the Albanians may allow the screening of Andrzej Wajda's *Man of Marble* (1976) and *Man of Iron* (1981), brilliant instances of the art documentary in which Polish realities and dreams of democracy are intermingled to produce a memorable synthesis worthy of the Golden Palm at Cannes. Until the Albanian film industry is permitted to divest itself of its political straitjacket, it will be unable to reveal the undoubted talents of its writers, directors, actors, and actresses.

3
Apollonia and Berat

Our departure from Durrës to Fier was held up by the late arrival of a new Albturist guide, Lejla, who was to take over the main responsibility for our good behaviour from Flora. Both were English-language schoolteachers from Tirana; their profession shone forth as they chided us from time to time on our proclivity for taking photographs without prior permission, or for wandering off without the necessary checking on our whereabouts. They gave explanations in English following the Albanian dictation of our driver, Koço, who had been a trusted employé of Albturist for fifteen years, and thus knew more of the countryside and the historic towns than our young guides, both in their twenties, could have been expected to learn. Their English was very good, considering that only medical and surgical specialists are permitted to study abroad.

We set out for Rrogozhinë and Fier at 8.30, reaching Fier at 10 a.m. after 82km. (Is Albanian the only language which can begin a word with double R?) The pleasantly-wooded countryside gives way to sandy beaches on the right of the road. In 8km., we see the Shkumb i Kavajës (Rock of Kavajë), where Caesar confronted Pompey in the Civil War of 49 B.C. Kavajë itself is a small town of some 12,000 people (as compared with 7,000 on liberation, in 1944) surrounding a ruined 18th-century mosque. Recorded in history for the first time in the 16th century, Kavajë can best be understood from its museum, in a characteristic house, with a hole in the roof as a chimney. The women used to spend their free time at home on needlework and pottery, but modern Kavajë now boasts factories for glass, carpets and paper. There are no names on the shop-fronts, but only descriptions: KINKALERI (the French 'quincaillerie', for cotton-reels, cigarettes, needles and suchlike), DYQANI LULEVE (Florist's), and FRUTA—PERIME (Fruit—Vegetables). Even here in the warm lowlands, red pantiled house-roofs slope against rain; we shall have to travel southward to Greece before flat roofs confidently stare up at blue skies.

On to Gosë, where even the state pig-farm is surrounded by concrete bunkers. Could they be manned in a trice by pig-keepers, shooting down pigs that try to escape? Wheat froths over the edge of the road, so our bus may brush it like a talisman as we rock past.

And now we arrive at the river Shkumbi, having passed Rrogozhinë, with its factories for cotton and soap. Scrubland gives way to olives and vines, but still stones weigh down many fields with the burden of history, and the clearance of boulders for agriculture is seen to be the one central task of labourers, volunteers, and those assigned to 'productive labour'. As a writer, I have often wondered what labour can be more productive than writing, but my misunderstanding of the term is wilful, when I know that 'hard manual labour' is what is really meant.

Lushnjë, the classical Marusium, is 55km. from Durrës. It is the seat of the Congress which met on 21 January 1920 to codify the democratic feelings of Albanians following the anti-Italian demonstration of Vlorë on 28 November 1919 and openly expressing fears aroused in Albania by the Paris Conference of 1919. The pro-Italian government based at Durrës was formally rejected, and Tirana chosen as the new capital. In 1970 the building where the Congress of Lushnjë had been held was turned into another museum devoted to patriotism. I personally find that more than two hours of unremitting patriotism gives me a headache, but others seem to find the exaltation of one's own nation above others (after all merely an extension of egotism) endlessly entertaining.

Ask instead to see the 18th-century icons in the church called Kisha e Shën e Premtës in Lushnjë. One is of St Nahum, and the other—far more interesting—is Constantine Shpataraku's *Last Supper*.

The 30km. road from Lushnjë to Fier traverses a lush landscape of small agricultural co-operatives and state farms. Near Kolonjë, on a cypress-girt hill, you will see the former monastery of Ardenicë, with an ex-church decorated with murals by Constantine Shpataraku and Athanasios, two monks from Korçë. The best work by the former portrays the feudal chief Karl Thopia.

Fier

Fier was founded by Omer Pasha Vrioni, whose family had for generations owned land in the vicinity. A virulent foe of the Greek Revolution of 1821 and its effects, Vrioni dreamed of a city that would serve as a market town for the commerce and agriculture of the Muzaki plains, and engaged the French architect Barthélemy to design a new town in the 1870s. Fier's grand avenues, shady even in the midday sun, lead to a square where a bronze bust of Stalin silently, and *almost* impassively gloats over the triumph of his steely allies against the feudal pashas like Vrioni.

Fier, the granary of Albania, has also become known as an industrial

Fier. View from the Hotel Apollonia to the main square.

centre, with a cotton mill, brick-factory, oil refinery, and chemical plant.
Though founded so recently, Fier already vies in its population of 30,000
with ancient Berat. We took Turkish coffee on the terrace outside the
Hotel Apollonia on the main square, and read the hoardings and
banners: DEMOKRACIA PROLETARE ESHTE DEMOCRACI E
VERTETE (Proletarian democracy is true democracy) and LAVDI
DESHMOREVE (Glory to the Martyrs). Less conspicuous billboards
advertised the films *Salammbô* and *Si gjithë të tjerët*, from 8.30 to 10.30.
Winter film shows are from 10 to 12.

I watched the faces of Albanians as they passed. Most were broad of
temple, with dark, wavy hair, their broad faces ending in an aggressively
jutting chin. The nose is moderately prominent, whether straight or
slightly curved or aquiline, and the eyes predominantly brown. Sallow
complexions due to malaria are found now only among the older
generations. A hard working life leads to premature ageing in both sexes;
in women there is a tendency to stoutness, especially since cakes are both
excellent and abundant. Children tend to be small and wiry, better in
stamina than their elders at the same age due to better food. Very few
Albanians seem to wear glasses, and their teeth look better than those in
capitalist countries.

I begged to visit the Public Library, and both Flora and Lejla kindly gave up an hour to come with me. For it is not enough to be able to ask questions in Albanian, understand the answers, and write them down. The Albturist guides are also there to ensure that you ask the correct questions and are given the correct answers, because so few Albanians ever meet a foreigner that they might answer in a way that may be objectionable.

One plaque outside the library is dedicated to Ismail Qemal (an aristocrat we know as Ismail Kemal Bey), born in January 1844 at Vlorë, where he was later to proclaim Albanian independence. His enthralling *Memoirs* were translated into English and published by Constable in 1920.

Another plaque honours Abdyl Frashëri (1839–92), curtly stating that he came to Fier in November 1878, though this is not his prime claim to celebrity. Earlier in 1878 Frashëri had set up the famous League of Prizren (now in Albanian-speaking Yugoslavia) with Mehmet Vrioni, the two men later being joined by Abdyl's younger brothers Naim (possibly the best-known Albanian poet of all), and the educator Sami.

Abdyl's son Midhat—who wrote as 'Lumo Skendo'—was a great Albanian patriot, defying the Turkish occupation and later the Nazi occupation, but he fell foul of the Communists by founding the right-wing Balli Kombëtar (literally 'National Front') and suffered the anguish of exile from independent Albania as well as from his subjugated nation. In numerous books and articles he had advocated marsh clearance, reduction or abolition of taxes, and industrialisation, but he was a man before his time. His great library of at least 18,000 volumes, many rare and valuable, was confiscated together with other major libraries, forming the nucleus of the modern National Library in Tirana's Palace of Culture.

Just as a nurse will judge a country by the quality of its nursing, or a chef by the quality of its cuisine, as a librarian I wanted to evaluate the Albanian library system, taking as a sample not the National Library, for no national library can be typical, but a public library like that of Fier. Serving an urban population of 30,000, it is housed in a splendid building which was evidently not purpose-built. The six staff (all ladies) claim a membership of 5,000, or one in six, including 2,000 children. The library is open from 9–12 and 4–8 on five days a week, 8–1 on Sundays, and closed on Mondays. Since the library (like all others in Albania) is closed to browsers, you must check the catalogue for specific books, and then ask for what you want. This discourages readers, but they do at least have access to a handful of newspapers and magazines in reading rooms upstairs with six tables and 24 chairs.

So few magazines are published in Albanian that it might seem natural

Fier. Public Library.

to display some foreign journals, but since these might contain sensitive material—and by their candour show up the vacuous optimism of local journals—the few foreign-language magazines which do enter Albania are restricted in use to trusted readers and university staff. The many books in Russian, including the works of Stalin, Lenin and more surprisingly Tolstoi and Turgenev, reveal like a geological stratum the doctrines and allegiances of past years: now Russian has been displaced, as the first foreign language taught in schools, by English. Runs of English-language scientific and technical journals, in medicine and engineering, for instance, end in 1970 or 1971, and are gathering dust. The Librarian, Shoqja Pavlina, acquires Albanian books from a state bookshop in Fier. The few foreign titles needed by local readers (such as technicians at the automated oil refinery which opened in 1968) can be obtained by inter-library loan from the National Library in Tirana, which acts as a central clearing-house: its *Information Bulletin for Foreign Literature* is sent to all public libraries once a month.

Adult readers may borrow books for two weeks at a time, then if they fail to return or renew books they pay a fine of 20 qindarkas a day for nine days, and 50 qindarkas a day for the tenth day onward (100 qindarkas = 1 lek = 8½ pence). A reader who loses a book must pay 5 times its cost. The Junior Library, frustratingly also on closed access, is available to all children between 7 to 15, and parents of younger children may choose books from the catalogue on their behalf.

All the staff members in Fier are graduates in literature with two years' library training and attendance at a variety of seminars. Their simplified Dewey Decimal Classification, and their reliance on the card catalogue rather than the stock, reveals a mentality dating back almost to the nineteenth century in the West, when readers were not allowed free access to their own books. A hundred thousand volumes are claimed to be behind these closed doors, and as I was privileged to examine the bookstacks and periodicals room, as well as the children's shelves, I might be persuaded to agree that if you added all the multiple copies of works by Comrade Enver to all issues of newspapers and magazines, you might come up with a total not far short of that comfortably round figure.

But libraries are not to be hidden behind closed doors—behind the stolid cards of an author, title and subject catalogue. A public library is for browsing, and for representing every shade of opinion on every conceivable subject. A notice-board at Fier announces such forthcoming library activities as 'A Discussion of the Rôle that Libraries can play in Propaganda' and 'Work for Proletarian Education'. A distinguished British Librarian, D.J. Foskett, once summed up the creed of a librarian in objectively serving the community as 'no politics, no religion, and no morals'. The reader may take his or her choice.

Official figures give the number of public libraries in 1978 as 46, with 3.4 million books, as against 39 in 1970 with 1.9 million books, 16 in 1960 with 0.7 million books, and 12 in 1950 with 0.2 million books.

Book production in Albania in 1978 was officially put at 934 titles in a total of 10.8 million copies, as opposed to 616 titles in 1970 totalling 7.3 million copies, 422 titles in 1960 totalling 2.8 million copies, 125 titles in 1950 totalling 1.4 million copies, and 61 titles in 1938 totalling 0.2 million copies.

A major hindrance to book production is the fact that no small publishers can publish books privately, without official authorisation, as happens in a democracy where freedom of speech and publication is practised. In the U.K. for example, only 360 publishing companies, of the 9,000 existing who have published one book or more, are members of the Publishers' Association, and thus likely to be large or fairly large. All the rest are small, private, independent and often quite idiosyncratic. In Albania, as in most Communist states, publishing is carefully controlled by the Party, and all jobs in authorship and publishing are reserved for those who can be trusted to keep the Party clean. But it is precisely the rebels who, as creators and intellectuals, must be allowed to push forward the frontiers of art and thought, spending their time on what may not yet (or ever) be acceptable.

43

Apollonia

As our coach rolled out of Fier towards the tiny Adriatic beach resort of Seman, we were all in a high good humour: chilly northerners awarded the Gold Medal of the sun. At a cross-roads we turned left beyond anti-aircraft guns to 'Pojan', the truncated Albanian form of 'Apollonia'.

Cities of the god Apollo abound: the one I love best is the port of Cyrene, and named Apollonia for the patron deity of Cyrene, now Shahhat. There are two Apollonias in Crete, another in Sicily not far from Cefalù, two in Macedonia, one in Thrace, and several more in Asia Minor, now Turkey. Illyrian Apollonia was a foundation of Corinthians and Corcyraeans (whom we now call Corfiotes) in the seventh century B.C., but the first record we have of their presence there is in 588. Originally called Gylakeia, after its founder Gylax (Thucydides tells us), it was renamed after its patron deity: coins of the fifth century B.C. already indicate 'Apollonia'. Though not a port, it lay near enough to the river Aoos (the modern Vjosë) and to the sea to develop good trading links with other Mediterranean and Adriatic cities. It seems to have been fortified with walls from the fourth century B.C.: its citadel and fortifications were well known to Caesar, who determined to seize it as a stronghold in his civil war against Pompey, and succeeded in so doing. Celebrated as a seat of Greek learning, Apollonia invited many Roman nobles and their sons. Augustus spent several months there with his friend Agrippa in the first century B.C., before he was called back to Rome on the death of his uncle (according to Suetonius). It is at this epoch that Cicero hails Apollonia as 'urbs magna et gravis' for the grandeur of its buildings and the splendour of its literary and philosophical reputation.

Apollonia declined in the third and fourth centuries A.D., at first gradually, and then catastrophically with the change of course by the river Aoos 10km. southward: Avlon (modern Vlorë) superseded Apollonia in strategic importance. The first feature of the ancient city to strike the eye is a remnant of the wall 4½km. long which surrounded the town, and was reinforced with towers at intervals. Drainage channels, still visible in several places, served to allow the rains to run away from the lower sectors of the town which would otherwise have been flooded.

A wall rising 100m. to the summit of the hill from the outer wall to the Stoa leads to the Temple of Artemis. A phallic symbol, the obelisk dedicated to Apollo, can be traced back to extant coins of the fourth century B.C.

The so-called Bouleterion, or Hall of the Agonothetes, was the centre of the city administration, where the council deliberated. The building dates from the 2nd century A.D., being dedicated by a high official,

Apollonia. Bouleterion.   Apollonia. Byzantine Church of
St Mary.

Quintus Vellius, to the memory of his brother, the soldier Vellius
Valentinus Furius Proculus. An article by Koço Zheku in *Monumentet* 18
(1979) shows the patient reconstruction of this graceful building from the
ground-plan and the excavations of the French Archaeological Mission
under Léon Rey (*Albania*, 1935), author of the first and best French-
language guide-book, *Guide de l'Albanie* (1930).

In front of the Bouleterion stands a ruined colonnade, behind which is
the ancient library, with niches for the papyrus rolls which served as city
records and books, and the Odeon of the third century B.C. built into the
hillside. Its benches to seat about 220 were covered with marble, like the
orchestra, arguing an aristocratic audience. The city would have
contained up to 40,000 people at this time, so an amphitheatre for the
masses must be somewhere in the nine-tenths of Apollonia still to be
excavated. After the Bouleterion, the most striking feature of Apollonia
so far unearthed is the fine portico of the fourth century B.C., about
75m. long (though originally 77) and 14m. wide. Seventeen niches would
have held statues of the gods or of leading citizens.

South of the portico you can find some houses and shops of the Roman
period in a street six to seven metres wide. A nearby House of Mosaics
dating to the third century A.D. clearly belonged to an affluent family.
Though the mosaics have none of the brilliance associated with coastal

sites of Tunisia or Piazza Armerina in Sicily, they are amusing enough, Nereids gambolling on dolphins, and Achilles carrying the (now missing) body of Penthesilea, wounded queen of the Amazons.

Try to find time for the Nymphaeum on the hillside, to which spring-water was led down. The monumental fountain may have been the inspiration for a worn terra-cotta in the museum showing a woman carrying an amphora on her head, a common enough sight until recently all over mountainous Albania.

The former Monastery and Church of Shën Mëri (St Mary) date from 1350. The beautiful little church is a jewel of Byzantine art, with a central dome on four columns. Most of the frescoes are missing: the only one I could still see shows Emperor Andronikos Paleologos, who may have commissioned the church. The narthex is later than the rest of the church. You will be fascinated by the gargoyles on the Romanesque-style capitals outside the church, one reminding me of that remarkable Stanley Spencer painting of 1920 *Christ Carrying the Cross*, where curtains fly out of the window as if they were wings on the figures leaning forward.

Apollonia. Icons in the Byzantine Church.

The icons, variable in quality, are riddled with woodworm, but glass has recently been fitted to protect them from vandals. One of the best of the icons is of John the Baptist: others portray the Dormition of the Virgin, Jesus in his usual hieratic stance in Byzantine iconography, and the Virgin with apparently-mature Child also very typical of the style. Outside the church a well proves its antiquity by the deep striations of ropes at its rim.

Our guide was not the well-loved Pilo described by previous travellers (he had died in the early 1970s) but a young man called Vangjel. It was he who mentioned the recent discovery of the amphitheatre that everyone realised must have existed: it seats up to 8,000 spectators. The Archaeological Museum has a gallery, two porticoes, and seven rooms which, as invariably in Albania, carry no legends in an international language (French would have been apppropriate, given the work of Léon Rey), and sell neither books nor postcards: there is not even a printed plan of Apollonia for you, dear reader: you must be content with my written description or go to study the sketchy plan in the first room of the museum. In Room 2 you will find some red-figure vases of the fifth century B.C. which might be Apulian. More red-figure vases are shown in Room 3, with a Battle of the Amazons in marble, an exquisite male torso, and a terra-cotta revealing the cult of the earth-goddess Demeter. Room 4 is notable for a wide range of terra-cottas, early coins, and bronze weapons of the third century B.C. Outstanding in Room 5 is an architectonic detail in stone: Atlas holding up the world, dated to the 2nd century B.C. Room 6 shows plaster casts and busts, including some copies of works in Tirana and overseas, since finds from Apollonia now also adorn museums in Naples, Paris and Vienna, though when I asked for examples from ancient Illyria I drew a blank in the British Museum. Room 7 has some splendid sculptures of heads. A gallery of full-length sculptures completes the tour, but it is worth retracing one's steps to examine again such treasures as the delicate bust of Billia (as late as the second or third centuries A.D.), and the powerfully intellectual head of Demosthenes, which may be roughly contemporary, and hence a Roman copy of a Greek original.

Before leaving this evocative site, rest under the spreading oak which has shaded visitors to Pojan for at least the last five centuries, and listen to a story told of Comrade Enver's visit to Apollonia some years ago. The farmers were becoming more and more incensed as archaeologists reserved more and more of 'their' land for scientific digging as opposed to fruitful agriculture and complained to the local and national authorities without success, the arbitrator from Tirana having gone back to the capital without a decision. Finally, Comrade Enver passed that way, and members of the co-operative went to greet him and to offer him a glass of raki. He said nothing but looked so preoccupied that, instead of putting their case, they asked what was troubling him. 'It's the people of Durrës and the archaeologists,' he sighed. 'Those devilish archaeologists want me to destroy the city of Durrës so that they can excavate ancient Dyrrhachion below'. 'Are you going to allow it?' asked the anxious peasants. 'What worries me is not the cost of demolition,' answered Comrade Enver, 'nor even the cost of building new houses to replace the old. No: it's the destruction of all those charming old houses that everyone likes and is used to'. 'But are you really going to allow all the houses to be pulled down?' repeated the sweating farmers of Pojan. 'Have we any choice?' responded the Secretary of the Party of Labour. 'We must uncover the glorious history of our Motherland.' And from that day to this, the farmers of Apollonia have not said a word against the archaeologists from Tirana...

Berat

The road inland from Apollonia to Fier to Berat is a distance of 42km., passing through Poshnje and Ura Vajgurore, a landscape like Wyoming, teeming with small oil derricks.

Berat's Hotel Tomori is named for the higher of its two mountains (2415m.), the lower being Shpirag (1213m.). The situation of the hotel, on a square high above the river Osum (classical Apsus), commands a stunning view of the gorge, across which Kurt Pasha ordered a great bridge to be built in 1780. Since they said it was impossible, he cast a bag of gold down into the torrent to prove that money was no object. Legend would have you believe that a woman was immured into the foundations of the bridge to insure against its collapse, but in the 1920s, when the bridge was being repaired, the tale was exposed: they did find a woman's head, but it was carved in wood!

The city was originally Illyrian, as one can see from the great blocks of stone at the base of the fortress walls. The Romans called it Antipatria, and Albanorum oppidum, Apustius having captured it in 200 B.C. when detailed to do so by Sulpicius during a campaign against Macedonia. In the early fifth century Theodosius II (408–50) strengthened the city, and renamed it Pulcheriopolis, after his sister Pulcheria. In the ninth century it became the seat of a bishop and in 1205 it was refortified by Michael Comnenos. The marauding Serbs under Stefan Dušan captured the place in 1345, renaming it Belgrad (like the modern capital of Yugoslavia, meaning 'White City'). It is a corruption of this name that gives us modern 'Berat'.

The local Balsha princes held Berat until the Turks seized it in 1450

Berat. Leaden Mosque (now Architectural Museum) and Monument.

(having lost ten thousand killed in a seven-month siege during 1438), and Skënderbeg was utterly routed in his attempt to win the city back. The Ottomans allowed native pashas and beys to rule on their behalf: not only Kurt of the bridge, and Ismail, but Ibrahim, who had to defend Berat against Ali Pasha of Tepelenë, and failed against a force of 5,000 men besieging under Omer Vrioni in 1809. Though Ali's *coup* was undertaken without prior authority from the Sublime Porte, Ali was quick to explain that he suspected Ibrahim Pasha of being in league with France, and thus a traitor to the Ottoman Empire. The Sultan thereupon appointed Ali's son Mukhtar as Governor of Berat, and the city was strengthened yet again.

A museum has been created in the building where the first session of the National Liberation Front (now the Democratic Front) was held on 20 October 1944. The Leaden Mosque (Xhamië e Plumbit) in the main square is now an architectural museum of surpassing interest, with photographs and plans of buildings throughout Albania, for Berat has been designated a 'museum-city' like Gjirokastër. The Leaden Mosque was originally constructed in 1553–5, but has been heavily restored. It is possible to climb the minaret with the approval of Myslim Hotova,

Director of Museums (tel. Berat 286), who also controls entry to the various churches in the citadel, which used to be without water and thus of greater artistic than military value. The old town is the former Muslim sector: More-Çelepi on the left bank of the Osúm, while the former Christian sector is Gorica (Serbo-Croat for 'little mountain'), on the right bank. The houses are built up in banks against the sides of the mountain, all their windows facing each other, out towards the river, as in Tripoli of Lebanon.

The citadel, with a fine new road leading down to Gorica, still shows the initials of Michael Comnenos (M K). Here is the Greek Orthodox cathedral, which reminded me of that passage in *Sons of the Eagle* (1937), where Ronald Matthews describes his visit to the episcopal palace.

'We were shown into the bishop's cool dark study, lined with Greek commentaries on the scriptures and books of Orthodox canon law. A little purple-clad chaplain, shining with heat and bearded, like a tousled apostle, received us . . . The bishop himself was tall, straight, thin, long-haired and long of face. His square black beard and steel-rimmed spectacles gave him the air of a Hebrew prophet—and of something else which I could not quite define. And then, as he composed himself in his wooden arm-chair, and folded his hands precisely and bent attentively towards us, I suddenly saw what that missing element was. It was a public school headmaster.'

The prophet-headmaster took Matthews to see his cathedral. 'It was small and dark and secretive, with that secretiveness one often feels in the lesser Orthodox churches, as if one had trespassed across the threshold of a forbidden rite. The blackened oak of its furnishings was so luxuriant that it seemed less to have been placed there than to be growing there. . . The pulpit sprouted from the stone flags to take shape as an enormous gilt wooden tulip, the twelve apostles following each other in a frozen march round its base.' Another fourteen of the churches were said to be still open for worship during the mid-1930s.

Once three hundred houses were inhabited inside the citadel, water being brought daily from the river up a staircase cut in the bare rock by means of a chain-gang with buckets. I wandered among the ramshackle houses and the restored churches, peeping over into jealously-tended private patches of garden, one with a little dog whose squeal sounded much worse than his bite. The Cathedral (ask for 'Kisha e Madhe' or Big Church) is halfway to the newly-constructed belvedere, with a restaurant, on the very brink of the citadel overlooking the plain. I chatted in Italian with an old lady in black not far from the stone house marked Familja Jorgji Bishka. Ask Comrade Myslim to show you the

Kisha Vangjelistra (Church of the Evangelists) of the sixteenth century, with the finest sequence of icons by Onufri.

Onufri's dates of birth and death are not known, but extant frescoes by him, datable to the mid-sixteenth century, can be found in Berat (St Theodore, in the citadel), and in two churches in Elbasan district (St Nicholas, Shelçan, Shpat, and the Church of Good Friday, Valësh), as well as in the Church of the Holy Apostles (founded by Giorgio Tzotzias), one of the thirty-one visible churches in Kastoria, Greece.

The first inscription recording Onufri's name was found in 1951, in the Shelçan church: 'Kur të ngresh duerët e tueja ke Perëndia, o meshtar i Perëndisë, më përmend edhe mue mëkatarin e të padhitunin piktor Onufrin'—'When you lift your hands to God, O priest of God, remember also me, the sinful and ignorant painter Onufri'. The Valësh church has two inscriptions which offer more information: a date of execution, 1554, and the words 'protopapë të Neokastrës'(protopope of Elbasan). The Kastoria church has a date: 23 July 1547, and a reference to Onufri's origin in Berat.

Theofan Popa, the leading scholar of mediaeval Albanian art, has suggested that Onufri, whose surname is not known, visited Italy, and broadened his horizon with Renaissance ideas of colour, line and vitality far removed from the mainstream of Byzantine stylization. Certainly he mastered the techniques of fresco and icon, introducing a certain realism, and a degree of individuality in facial expression, though these two characteristics were then considered dispensable. A tablecloth

Berat. House and garden
in the Old City.

embroidered in traditional Albanian style, a gourd (in the Nativity at Shelçan) used by a shepherd as a water-bottle as it still is today in country districts, and horses' tails tied in a manner peculiar to Albania: all these are features which mark Onufri out as a personality worth study. Onufri uses violet for the rocks in the foreground of the Shelçan Descent into Limbo, and dark grey for Limbo itself. Elsewhere he chooses lilac, orange, cherry, maroon, vermilion, and turquoise to offset the traditional gold.

Onufri was the greatest of the sixteenth-century painters in Albania, and he founded the School of Berat, which was to establish his style and methods not only in Berat but in what one must be tempted to call Greater Albania, including parts of modern Yugoslavia and Greece (where of course the churches are nowadays more freely visible).

In Berat's Church of St Mary Blacherna there is an inscription 'Dhe piktori Nikolla biri i Onufrit, vjeti 1578' (And the painter was Nikolla, son of Onufri, in the year 1578). Another certain attribution to Nikolla is the work in the Church of St Nicholas, Kurjan, near Fier. Most of the School of Berat artists were anonymous, and much of their work has been lost, but we do know the names of Joan and Onufri the Cypriot, as well as Nikolla.

St Mary Blacherna demonstrates the typically didactic nature of Byzantine art in an illiterate community: the pictures are there to tell the Biblical stories, and to identify (however spuriously) the faces of the apostles and the saints, Jesus and Mary. Onufri's Nativity, Presentation at the Temple, and Resurrection of Lazarus, all in the Church of the Evangelists, served to illustrate the priest's words as well as to keep Biblical images and phrases in the worshipper's mind. So did the much earlier icon of St Nicholas in the Church of St George, and a fresco of St Laurence which might be by Onufri in the Church of St Theodore.

Frescoes in the Church of the Holy Trinity suffered from the church's use as a powder-magazine during the Turkish occupation. The classical pillars and capitals, of Roman date, had been pillaged from pagan temples, and now Albania has returned to the anti-religious fervour of Trajan's times. For Nero and for Comrade Enver alike, Christians are trouble-makers and dissidents who must be silenced. Things were different eighty years ago. The French traveller Ravier reported that the head of a village on the Black Drin river was Catholic, his brother Muslim, and interdenominational marriages were frequent. On Sundays some Muslims attended Mass!

When Justin Godart visited Berat's Church of St Demetrios in 1921, he found six people pulling it down for building materials. The choir had been demolished and they were starting on the nave. M. Godart called

Berat. Byzantine Church of St Michael.

the mayor, who caught them slashing five century-old frescoes with their pickaxes. I thought wryly of the motto of the Party of Labour of Albania, which took power as the Communist Party twenty-three years after M. Godart's visit, 'To build socialism holding a pickaxe in one hand and a rifle in the other'.

Down below the citadel stands the tiny church of St Michael near the cliff-edge, with its neighbour St Constantine.

There are only two important mosques in Berat apart from the Leaden Mosque in the main square (where the buses and taxis stop): a delightful minaret pierces the sky on the citadel not far from the new restaurant, and the Xhamië e Beqarëvet (Bachelors' Mosque), with its slim minaret seeming to rise out of water direct to the sky.

Not far from the Hotel Tomori stands the fine new Palace of Culture, where performances of a film based on Ugo Betti's *Corruzione nel Palazzo di Giustizia* had been given a few days earlier. A translation into Albanian of the play had been printed in 4,000 copies in Tirana.

Blue-overalled women in the local bookshop were unwrapping new copies of volume 36 (June-October 1967) of the Works of Comrade Enver to add to the rows of the other thirty-five volumes already on the laden shelves. I bought a historical atlas of Albania well-produced for schools in Tirana ten years earlier, and the morning paper *Zëri i Popullit*.

I asked permission to attend the evening performance of *Dy krisma në Paris* (*Two Shots in Paris*), a play by Sheri Mita and Pëllumb Kulla, at the Teatri i Shtëpisë Kulturës M. Tutulani, not far from our hotel. Lejla and Flora accompanied a handful of us, and kindly interpreted in whispers. The subject of the play is the assassination of Esat Pasha Toptani, an Albanian politician now regarded as a traitor, by the Communist Avni Rustemi. Set in 1920, the play's first scene shows an idealistic youth being shot by forces of the Italian occupation. On 3 June 1920, following the Congress of Lushnjë, the Albanian national government demanded the withdrawal of Italian troops from Vlorë, thus clearing the country of all occupying troops. Hundreds of Albanians left their villages and towns to join in the battle for Vlorë and, though many lost their lives, victory was achieved. The Paris Conference being held in June was being attended by representatives of the pro-Italian groups led by Esat Pasha Toptani.

Act II shows the intrigue of Esat Pasha, and his assassination on 13 June by Avni Rustemi, who was to lead the anti-Zogist Bashkimi (Union) organization.

Act III is set in the court-room in Paris, where Rustemi is being tried for murder. Witnesses true and false testify, to the increasing excitement of the audience, whose emotions rise to fever-pitch as the verdict is announced. Counsel for the defence, Anatole de Monzie, emphasised that this was not a cynical or venal crime, but 'a crime of passion, premeditated by a whole people'. Esat Pasha and his employés could not be protected by diplomatic immunity, for it was now clear that the so-called government of Selenicë did not represent the people at all: the capital of Albania was now Tirana. Rustemi was acquitted, but we should add a postscript to the play: on 20 April 1924 Avni Rustemi was himself murdered in Tirana, an event which either directly or indirectly led to a rising against Zog and his right-wing allies, who were forced to flee abroad.

The acting throughout was exceptionally fine, though the players were amateurs. One could isolate the warm personality of Thoma Rrapi, as old Xhafo Mehmeti, and Ardian Cerga as the ardent young Rustemi, but the excellent ensemble could hardly be faulted in any detail. The auditorium may be plain, but the costumes are striking in their authenticity, and a revolving stage adds a touch of professionalism. Albanian theatres have no interval for coffee or drinks, but just a slight pause between acts. Evening performances start at about 7 and finish between 8.30 and 9. The theatre manager kindly offered me a poster, in the absence of a programme, and the actors stayed behind to autograph it: we few foreigners formed a guard of honour outside the theatre to applaud the cast as they emerged, a gesture they clearly appreciated. The style and content of Albanian plays are, like the films, almost exclusively ideological. The first professional theatre was the People's Theatre founded in May 1945 under the Yugoslav Boza Nikolić, a few months after the Revolution. The earliest performances included the Yugoslav play *The Lover* and translations from the Russian, but these were dropped from the repertory after the rupture with the Soviet Union in favour of Albanian plays. The second theatre was set up in Shkodër in 1949 and the third at Korçë in 1950.

According to the Autumn 1977 issue of *Albanian Life*, 'The Albanian theatre has always [*sc.* since 1945] reflected the revolutionary reality in socialist Albania: the demands of the working class and the cooperativist peasantry to consolidate the new society'. Hence such nationalistic plays as Kolë Jakova's *Toka Jonë (Our Land)*, on agrarian reform; *The Prefect* by Besim Lëvonja, against Fascist collaborators; and *The Peasant Girl* by Fatmir Gjata, extolling the life of a working girl in the Stalin Textile Mill. Official figures give the number of theatres in Albania in 1978 as 27 with 8,759 seats, as against 25 in 1970 with 7,132 seats, 18 in 1960 with 4,614 seats, and only 4 in 1950 with 1,332 seats.

Stylised political drama ('realism' is an odd word to describe tableaux vivants lit rosy-pink) does not play to packed houses in Albania, any more than it does anywhere else, but the price of a ticket averages no more than 3 leks (about 25 pence) in the towns, while admission costs nothing in some rural districts. There is little else to do in the evenings apart from go to bed early, for cinemas are rare, and the local Palace of Culture may offer no alternative to the evening's routine *passeggiata* up and down the main street.

Just as the promenade is a movement of the massed people, without leaders, so the political drama of Albania unfolds on a stage without stars. The audience is supposed to repeat the slogans on the stage: pauses are stage-managed to enhance this effect. Everything is positive, optimistic, handsome and one-sided: the young Communist is healthy, fit, and brave. His opponent, whether landlord, priest, enemy soldier or local traitor, is a sneering, sly, slouching coward. We are close to the spirit of Quilp, Uriah Heep, and Scrooge here, for as in Dickens the Copperfields and Twists of Albania always win. The difference is that in literary terms a hundred years have gone by, and Victorian melodrama should not be in the ascendant anywhere. We have grown up with the humanism of Faulkner, Kafka, Pasternak, Camus, Joyce, and Gabriel García Márquez, yet none of them can be found in Albanian bookshops. Gorki is still available in translation, and the plays of Shakespeare are now considered 'safe', but the other major writers of the world, from Sophocles and Terence to Goethe and Dostoevsky, are sadly absent.

Berat. Sign-writers at work in the cobbled street.

Everything is simply good or simply bad, depending on its relationship to Albania's interpretation of Marxism-Leninism according to Stalin and Mao. The Albanian view is drastically easy to comprehend: there is only one correct ideology. The capitalists have never understood or wished to understand it. The Yugoslav, Soviet and Chinese revisionists once understood it, but now resort to pragmatism and expediency as opposed to rigid adherence to principle.

Christopher Hill, an English Marxist, has written that the Russian Revolution 'uplifted the poor and the downtrodden and improved their lot in the everyday things of life. This is what most impresses in contemporary records of the revolution, and this is what is likely to be its most widespread and lasting effect. For the everyday things of life still mean most to the poor and downtrodden, and they are still the majority of the population of the world.'

There can be no doubt that the masses in the Soviet Union are materially better off than they were in 1914, but then the same applies with much greater effect to the masses in capitalistic Western Europe and Japan, as well as to 'revisionist' Yugoslavia and China. And if the material wellbeing of the masses is the criterion of political success, can Albania claim that its particular brand of hard-line Stalinism has achieved success in relative terms?

The former Mao Tse-tung Textile Mill in Berat, inaugurated during the 3rd Five-Year Plan in 1966 with Chinese funds, experts, and machinery, is now known as the Organizatës së Rinisë të Filaturës të Kombinatët të Tekstilëve Berat. To me it seemed a living inferno of noise, but the 7,500 workers (most of them women) seemed to withstand the permanent din quite equably. The safety precautions seem hopelessly inadequate: nobody even wears a mask. A day is paid as three shifts of eight hours, though only seven hours are worked.

Pay runs from 500–700 leks (£42–£62) per month, women retiring at fifty and men at sixty, with an annual holiday averaging 21 days. Only local raw cotton was processed up to 1980, but from then on synthetic fibres have been introduced as well, imported from Yugoslavia, Italy and elsewhere, processed here, and in the main re-exported, to Bulgaria, Sweden, Italy and elsewhere.

Textile workers possess their own cinema club, drama group, subsidized canteen, crèche and kindergarten. Five doctors and a nursing team are available for emergencies. A criticism group may be formed if a worker's output is inadequate, and further punishment might include a place on the 'tortoise' half of the public notice-board, next to the high achievers of the 'jet-plane' half. Political information is given on Tuesdays, whereas a union meeting is held only once a month. This factory fulfilled its last six-month plan twenty-four days early... Most other official figures run smoothly and optimistically off the director's tongue... Union fees are 2 leks (17 pence) per month or 3 leks if the worker's pay is higher than 700 leks per month.

'The immediate cause of the present distress is the depreciation of human labour occasioned by machinery. Many are turned from work and face starvation. I propose therefore to establish Villages of Co-operation founded upon the principle of united labour. Here, men and women will work together in fellowship and finally prosper, for each will produce more than he or she or their family will consume. The fruit of their produce they will share in common'.

This is not the Voice of the Party of Labour of Albania—though you might be forgiven for thinking so by its tone—but of Robert Owen (1771–1858), whose co-operative villages in Scotland (New Lanark) and the U.S.A. (New Harmony) did not spark off the movement he so passionately advocated, even early in the Industrial Revolution. How anachronistic and anatopistic the co-operatives are today, as we move into the advanced electronic age, may be to some extent a matter of personal judgment; but such villages depend on the outside world's assistance for such matters as transport, defence, higher education, and communications, and in post-Maoist China communes are being quietly abolished, leaving Albania as the sole advocate of total State control.

I tried to forget the sallow faces of the women putting empty bobbins on roaring machines, taking off the full ones, putting on empty bobbins, taking off full ones. Automation would mean that fewer women would be employed in the factory, but could they not be found more rewarding jobs elsewhere? Could understand what you meant if you explained that the dictatorship of the proletariat meant they should be dictators, not dictated to? Did they ever contemplate a strike, for shorter hours, better working conditions, higher pay? Could nationalistic communism be the opium of the people? I escaped into the light of day, rejoicing selfishly that I lived in the twentieth century in a free country where pluralism had taken the place of bigotries, and where trade unions and religious organizations, political parties and warring heterodoxies are not only allowed but actually protected by a complex network of laws and regulations.

4
Vlorë and Gjirokastër

On the 34km. road from Fier to Vlorë the usual yoked-bullock carts induced our driver to veer across the road, hooting impatiently like any Neapolitan. We crossed the Vjosë at Mifol, and near Nartë saw on our left the lake of Nartë which has given salt from its salt-pans since time immemorial. Just before Vlorë we passed productive vineyards and then immense olive groves; inside the town oleanders turned even the dustiest roads a flattering pink.

Vlorë

Ancient Avlon (the word means 'a hollow between hills') is known from Greek coins of about 400 B.C. Important for its harbour, salt, and the olives celebrated by the Spanish-born Martial in the first century A.D., Avlon gave succour to Caesar in the Civil War against Pompey, and replaced Apollonia and Oricum as the chief port of Illyria. Wrecked time and time again by marauders, the city was eventually abandoned by its inhabitants, who moved a few kilometres south to modern Vlorë (Vlona in Geg Albanian, and Valona in Italian). In the Middle Ages Vlorë sought assistance from the fortress of Kaninë (ancient Chaonia), on the northern foothills of Mal i Çikës about 5km. southeast of Vlorë, so that invaders such as the Normans and Venetians were compelled to subdue Kaninë before they could lay siege to Vlorë.

Charles of Anjou held Vlorë from 1266 to 1372, but the Byzantines retook it under Andronikos II.

In 1417 Ottoman forces took Vlorë, Kaninë and Berat, General Hamza Bey becoming commander-in-chief of Vlorë, the first Adriatic port won by the Porte. He began to build ships there to defend the Adriatic coast and to undertake forays against the Venetians and against the coast of Apulia, only 75km. away. In the seventeenth century the fortress of Vlorë was endowed with new walls, high, thick, and plentifully bastioned. Suleiman the Magnificent ordered a mosque and a tower to be erected within the fortress, possibly commissioning his great architect Sinan with the job. The celebrated Turkish traveller Evliya Çelebi

(1611–84) left a fine description of contemporary Vlorë in his *Tarihi seyyah* (translated by Babinger in his *Rumelische Streifen*), and other accounts have been written by François Pouqueville, W.M. Leake, Sir Henry Holland, Heuzey, Weigand and Patsch.

In 1812 the notorious Ali Pasha of Tepelenë took Vlorë: exactly a century later Ismail Qemal Bey proclaimed Albanian independence by seceding from the Ottoman Empire. Subsequently declared a 'hero city' by the Communist Government for being the seat of the first (non-Communist) Albanian Government, Vlorë was captured in 1914 by the Italians, who held it until 1920.

Vlorë is now Albania's principal naval base and second port. Near the town centre are the Archaeological-Ethnographic Museum, and the Museum of Independence, and the two theatres, but the main square is dominated by a graceful sixteenth century mosque (now converted into an artist's studio) with a minaret, and the Independence Monument of 1972, a monstrous example of Soviet-inspired statuary in the full-blown style for some reason called 'Socialist Realism'.

You will be driven up to the hill above Vlorë for a panorama of the city with its verdant necklace and Adriatic horizon radiant in the sunlight. Here too, looming above the martyrs' graves, which deserve a more serene and graceful monument, is a huge cluster of figures more than life-size, in melodramatic poses showing grim determination.

From the belvedere we enjoyed a remarkable view over the plain of Vlorë, factory chimneys belching smoke which did not seem depressing,

Vlorë. Former mosque in the city centre, now an artist's studio.

as it would in a grey northern sky, but encouraging, as though men had set down their roots in a scene worthy of Delphi's gods and centaurs. (On the way down, however, this optimistic mood was tempered by finding the old Decauville narrow-gauge railway from the bitumen mine at Selenicë to the port of Skele overgrown with weeds and long disused.)

Vlorë. Martyrs' Monument, above the city.

Large capitals on the monument proclaim:

NEN UDHEHEQJEN E PARTISE,   (Under the leadership of the Party,
ME JU NE ZEMER,   always with you in our hearts,
MARSHOJME   we march on
GJITHMONE PERPARA,   ever forward
DUKE BERE REALITET   realizing
IDEALET, PER TE CILAT   the ideals, for which
JU NUK KURSYET AS JETEN   you laid down your lives)

61

The artists were obviously and wholly inspired by the prevailing Soviet artistic dogma which decrees—even now, in the complexity of modern life, with its teeming problems capable of multiple solutions—that (in the words of the Albanian Gent Arbana, *Les Lettres Albanaises*, no.1, 1980) 'Socialist Realism possesses such internal strength that it can tackle in all their aspects all themes from that of proletarian revolution to the most ancient legends.' As for its aims, far from being considered an art form capable of being judged on its own merits, it is a merely political instrument which, again to quote Comrade Gent, 'will definitively liquidate the cultural empire of the bourgeois and the revisionists.'

Or, taking the view of Peter and Linda Murray in *A Dictionary of Art and Artists*, 'Socialist realism is the official Party Art of the U.S.S.R. and the Communist Party generally. This is the dreariest kind of academic art, glorifying the Party or the Peasant and other stock figures. A victim has said of it: "Impressionism is painting what you see, Expressionism is painting what you feel, and Socialist Realism is painting what you hear".' In my opinion, the propaganda statues of Albanian Communism are no more valid as art than the optimistic, flag-waving platitudes of the daily newspaper *Zëri i Popullit* can be considered responsibly-balanced journalism in the style of *The Washington Post*, *The Times* or *Die Neue Zürcher Zeitung*.

When a serious critic like the Marxist Ernst Fischer tries to reconcile the claims of art and Communism, he is clearly uneasy. In *The Necessity of Art* (1963), Fischer urges a socialist 'art' (he too baulks at the spurious notion that 'realism' may be involved), but despairs at the ways in which the commissars have foisted *Kitsch* on generations of workers, and deplores the Socialist insistence on idealising a notional 'simple' man, as though the masses were not made up of a lot of different individuals. 'It is part of the irresistible advance of Socialism', he suggests, unconvincingly and obviously unconvinced, 'that the 'simple' man gradually turns into a subtle and highly differentiated man.' But where is the art that will enable him to achieve this subtlety, these aspirations? Not in the bombastic rifle-toting statues of the Soviet Union or Albania, but in Sung China, Mughal India, fifth-century B.C. Athens, Renaissance Florence, and above all in the spirited innovations of the European twentieth century: in Picasso, Henry Moore, Brancusi, Naum Gabo, or Giacometti.

Yet Ernst Fischer must not be dismissed as a Party hack, for his own particular view of art in a fully Communist world—if we were ever to have one—is that the individual and the collective are no longer in conflict. He finds this conflict in capitalistic art (which may be questionable) and in contemporary Socialism (which is not at all questionable). As opposed to present Socialist art, which he defines as 'a simple means of enlightenment and propaganda' (as though the two were somehow connected!), he predicts the emergence of an infinite variety of styles as the individual is reborn in a classless society. 'The permanent function of art,' insists Fischer, 'is to recreate *as every individual's experience* the fullness of *all that he is not*, the fullness of humanity at large... All art has to do with this identification, with this infinite capacity of man for metamorphosis, so that, like Proteus, he can assume any form and lead a thousand lives without being crushed by the multiplicity of his experience... Art as the means of man's identification with his fellow-men, nature and the world, as his means of feeling and living together with everything that is and will be, is bound to grow as man himself grows in stature.' It is hard to see, however, that Communism is better placed as a central philosophy to achieve these aims than Socialism, Liberalism or Conservatism.

The Hotel Adriatik in Vlorë stands unromantically opposite the Cold Store, a few minutes walk west of the town centre. It has a wonderful garden, with wild-looking flowers admirably trained and trimmed to simulate a brilliant wilderness. Roses and oleanders delight the eye under shady trees, with shafts of light arrowing on to well-watered flower-beds.

At mid-day I walked past the Historic Museum and the stadium of the soccer club Flamurtari Vlorë (the name means 'Standard-Bearers'), then explored the area of the Palace of Culture, where a patient donkey stood in the shade, and five urchins played football on a bare patch of land with all the intensity of a World Cup match.

Wandering from one dozing afternoon shop to the next I marvelled at the shortage of meat in a fertile area where sheep and cows could find such excellent grazing, and at the limited range of fruit and vegetables compared with any Western country which imports foodstuffs. Then I corrected myself: vegetarians are probably no worse off than beefeaters, and why spend valuable currency on buying more exotic fruits when those you already grow possess all the necessary vitamins?

The total absence of traffic in the main street sent a shiver down my back, as though I were the sole survivor of a holocaust which had by some quirk of permutation atomized all internal combustion engines and humans of Albanian origin. I patted a locked bicycle fraternally as it stood lonely in a rack, and then, crazy for traffic, ran up and down the road to enliven the melancholy dust. At a street-corner, a traffic policeman in blue whistled furiously at me: I must have been running on the wrong side of the road.

The Coast Road to Sarandë

Take the coast road to Sarandë if you can—the Riviera of Flowers—as the bumpy way winds through rough-hewn tunnels and high along cliffs within perennial sight of the glittering blue Adriatic and miles of unspoilt beaches, past Sazan Island.

Sazan is situated in the bay of Vlorë, 9km. offshore. Five kilometres from north to south, and 1½km. from west to east, its outline can be seen as two conical limestone hills about 350m. high, meeting in a low saddle. These hills form a separated continuation of the Karaburun peninsula which virtually encloses Vlorë Bay. Low scrub covers the island (the classical Sanson), and cliffs make the approaches menacing except at the Bay of S. Nicolò, with charted depths from 4—8m. Sazan was an important strategic point for the Italian colonialists, who stipulated that they should keep the island even after they had handed back the rest of the country, despite the lack of water, which was ferried over regularly from the spring at Uji i Ftohtë ('Cold Water'), just south of Vlorë on the road south to Sarandë. The Russians built and used a naval base on Sazan, but evacuated it in 1961.

In a few kilometres you will arrive by way of Vlorë's Orange Tree Avenue and lovely beaches at Uji i Ftohtë (Cold or Fresh Water). This is a seaside settlement where workers enjoy dormitories and other holiday facilities all the year round. The cliff road runs parallel to the grey slopes of the Karaburun peninsula. Where Karaburun meets the mainland there is Orik (classical Oricum), a settlement once rivalling Apollonia. Some remains from Oricum are found in the Archaeological Museum of Vlorë. Bathers were snorkelling: only one in 15 or 20 were women, wearing decorous one-piece swimsuits. The puritanical morals of Albania will strike some as too restrictive and others as entirely appropriate. Women wear hardly any make-up, use drab shades and conventionally-cut clothes to the point of making a cult of plainness and uniformity. Men wear simply-cut shirts and trousers, and put on jackets only in the cool of the evening: ties are worn only by dignitaries on ceremonial occasions.

Thirty-one km. from Vlorë you arrive at the village of Dukat, which marks the boundary between the Adriatic Sea to the north, and the Ionian to the south. Now the road, which is a disgrace to Albania, rises to the summit of the Pass of Llogorë (1,000m. high), before descending to Palasë (350m.) and to Dhërm (170m.). The last is probably the finest beach in Albania, and there is a memorably comic moment in Jan Myrdal's *Albania defiant* (1978) when the author arrives at Dhërm and asks for a night's lodging. He is refused and, on asking why, he is told that Dhërm is for the exclusive use of Albanian workers and no foreigner is permitted to sleep there. But why not make an exception for one tourist for one night? 'Because we cannot make exceptions for one, because if you make an exception for one you would have to make an exception for two, then four, then eight, then sixteen, then thirty-two, then sixty-four, then a hundred and'. . . Jan Myrdal, as pro-Albanian as the present writer, perceived (if dimly) the crazy logic of all this, and crept, chastened, back into the night. . .

Near Dhërm you might be able to persuade your guide to stop at the Church of St Mary for the mediaeval frescoes. Then again, you might not.

Thirteen km. beyond Dhërm you arrive at Himarë, settled from Corfu at roughly the same time as the Corfiote expansion elsewhere on to the Adriatic shores. Philip V of Macedon attacked Himarë, then known as Chimarra ('ravine' in Greek) in 214 B.C., and we have records too of the Roman contact in 167 B.C. as the legions marched back from their campaign in Macedonia. We know of a bishopric there at least as early as the ninth century, and a successful siege by the Bulgars in the tenth century. The Ottoman Empire with all its might captured little Himarë during the sixteenth century, but with allies such as Venice, Spain, Naples and even for a while Muscovy, the brave men of Himarë finally expelled the Turks in 1570, and thereafter were 'gracefully' exempted from paying taxes and tribute to Constantinople. Ali Pasha of Tepelenë took the town for a while in 1810 and then again in 1816—7, when sixty-two churches were listed. The Greek Orthodox church was always powerful in Himarë, and the clergy a powerful patriotic stimulus against Muslim Turks.

Like Durrës, Vlorë and Sarandë, the harbour of Himarë was improved by the Soviet Union during the Stalin era, then leased for sixty-six years by the Chinese under Mao Tse-tung. But it was a mistake by the West (and possibly by others?) to consider Albania an *ally* of the Soviet Union or China in purely military terms. In an interview with Leslie Gardiner, the diplomat Misto Treska stated: 'We do not have, and never have had, allies in the military sense of the term. China is not our ally [this at the height of Chinese influence in the late 1960s]. We have comrades who have chosen the same Socialist way, that is all.'

The district of Himarë includes not only Dhërm (from 'drymades', 'oakwoods' in Greek) but also Vuno ('the hill' in Greek), both in easily-defensible positions. Olives are cultivated, and fishing is a common occupation for local men.

Sarandë lies another 60km. to the south of Himarë beyond ancient Panormus (known to the Italians as Porto Palermo), Qeparo, Borsh, Piqeras, Lukovë and Shënvasi.

Inland to Sarandë

We took the mountain road from Vlorë to Sarandë via the historic city of Gjirokastër, where we were to stay. Our route lay through Fier and oil-rich Patos: the zone of Mallakastër continues as far as Ballsh, now a rail terminus. The ancient Byllis is not here but a little westward, below the modern village of Hekal. Where oil has been found, old-fashioned derricks abound; elsewhere the soil is used for fruit and vegetable crops if it is fertile enough. Everywhere, like stolid pawns in a huge chess-game, the slit-eyed bunkers prepare for war in the twentieth century, twenty-first, twenty-second... Overgrown as they are, their concrete is ageless and immune to corrosion. They will endure when all parties are over. PARTI ENVER is cut on limestone outcrops. Each village vies with its neighbours in providing a prominent position for the crimson banners lettered in black LAVDI PPRSH banners (Glory to the Party of Labour of the Republic of Albania). A frightened dog slips into a field. Women pick vegetables near the village of Qesarat, bent over in communal labour under the grinning, grilling sun. We enter Tepelenë, above the confluence of Drino and Vjosë, the classical Antigonea or Anticonia being at nearby Lekël. The population of the town has fluctuated enormously with the town's changing fortunes; in 1903 it was barely a thousand, the majority Muslims, whereas in the period of Ali Pasha and today it is nearly ten times that figure. The Fortress of Ali Pasha replaced a mediaeval castle: his palace regrettably no longer stands. But the memory of Byron does: with a plaque on the fortress wall, and an Albanian version of *Childe Harold* on sale in the bookshop.

Lord Byron was in Albania in 1809, the year which saw the publication of his *English Bards and Scotch Reviewers*. Arriving in Yannina, the capital of Epirus, he found that its ruler Ali Pasha was with his army in Illyria, besieging Ibrahim Pasha in Berat. Greatly to Byron's gratification, the commandant in Yannina had been told by Ali Pasha to provide the important foreigner with a house and all necessary supplies, but Byron determined to meet his host, 'one of the most powerful men in the Ottoman Empire'.

He set out from Yannina, and in nine days had reached Ali Pasha's stronghold of Tepelenë. Byron himself takes up the story in a letter to his mother dated from Prevesa (Northern Greece), 12 November 1809. 'Our journey was much prolonged by the torrents that had fallen from the mountains, and intersected the roads. I shall never forget the singular scene on entering Tepaleen at five in the afternoon, as the sun was going down. It brought to my mind (with some change of *dress*, however) Scott's description of Branksome Castle in his *Lay [of the Last Minstrel*, Canto I], and the feudal system. The Albanians, in their dresses (the most magnificent in the world, consisting of a long *white kilt*, gold-worked cloak, crimson velvet gold-laced jacket and waistcoat, silver-mounted pistols and daggers), the Tartars with their high caps, the Turks in their vast pelisses and turbans, the soldiers and black slaves with the horses, the former in groups in an immense large open gallery in front of the palace, the latter placed in a kind of cloister below it, two hundred steeds ready caparisoned to move in a moment, couriers entering or passing out with despatches, the kettle-drums beating, boys calling the hour from the minaret of the mosque, altogether, with the singular appearance of the building itself, formed a new and delightful spectacle to a stranger. I was conducted to a very handsome apartment, and my health inquired after by the vizier's secretary *à la mode turque*.'

'The next day,' continues Byron, 'I was introduced to Ali Pacha. I was dressed in a full suit of staff uniform, with a very magnificent sabre, etc. The vizier received me in a large room paved with marble; a fountain was playing in the centre; the apartment was surrounded by scarlet ottomans. He received me standing, a wonderful compliment from a Mussulman, and made me sit down in his right hand. I have a Greek interpreter for general use, but a physician of Ali's named Femlario, who understands Latin, acted for me on this occasion. His first question was, why, at so early an age [Byron was 21], I left my country?—(the Turks have no idea of travelling for amusement). He then said, the English minister, Captain Leake, had told him I was of a great family, and desired his respects to my mother; which I now, in the name of Ali Pacha, present to you. He said he was certain I was a man of birth, because I had small ears, curling hair, and little white hands, and expressed himself pleased with my appearance and garb. He told me to consider him as a father whilst I was in Turkey, and said he looked on me as his son. Indeed, he treated me like a child, sending me almonds and sugared sherbet, fruit and sweetmeats, twenty times a day... His highness is sixty years old, very fat, and not tall, but with a fine face, light blue eyes, and a white beard; his manner is very kind, and at the same time he possesses that dignity which I find universal among the Turks. He has the appearance of anything but his real character, for he is a remorseless tyrant, guilty of the most horrible cruelties, very brave, and so good a general that they call him the Mahometan Buonaparte... He called my Albanian soldier, who... like all the Albanians, is brave, rigidly honest, and faithful; but they are cruel, though not treacherous, and have several vices but no meannesses. They are, perhaps, the most beautiful race, in point of countenance, in the world; their women are sometimes handsome also, but they are treated like slaves, *beaten*, and, in short, complete beasts of burden; they plough, dig, and sow. I found them carrying wood, and actually repairing the highways.'

And in the second Canto of *Childe Harold's Pilgrimage*, Byron's view of Tepelenë, and its impressive river (Laos, now called Vjosë) is set to Spenserian verse:

> The sun had sunk behind vast Tomerit,
> And Laos wide and fierce came roaring by;
> The shades of wonted night were gathering yet,
> When, down the steep banks winding warily,
> Childe Harold saw, like meteors in the sky,
> The glittering minarets of Tepalen,
> Whose walls o'erlook the stream; and drawing nigh,
> He heard the busy hum of warrior-men
> Swelling the breeze that sigh'd along the lengthening glen.

> He pass'd the sacred Haram's silent tower,
> And underneath the wide o'er-arching gate
> Survey'd the dwelling of this chief of power,
> Where all around proclaim'd his high estate.
> Admidst no common pomp the despot sate,
> While busy preparation shook the court,
> Slaves, eunuchs, soldiers, guests, and santons wait;
> Within, a palace, and without, a fort:
> Here men of every clime appear to make resort.

> Richly caparison'd, a ready row
> Of armed horse, and many a warlike store,
> Circled the wide extending court below;
> Above, strange groups adorn'd the corridore;
> And oft-times through the area's echoing door,
> Some high-capp'd Tartar spurr'd his steed away:
> The Turk, the Greek, the Albanian, and the Moor,
> Here mingled in their many-hued array,
> While the deep war-drum's sound announced the close of day.

> The wild Albanian kirtled to his knee,
> With shawl-girt head and ornamented gun,
> And gold-embroider'd garments, fair to see:
> The crimson-scarfed men of Macedon;
> The Delhi with his cap of terror on,
> And crooked glaive; the lively, supple Greek:
> And swarthy Nubia's mutilated son;
> The bearded Turk, that rarely deigns to speak,
> Master of all around, too potent to be meek,

Are mix'd conspicuous: some recline in groups,
Scanning the motley scene that varies round;
There some grave Moslem to devotion stoops,
And some that smoke, and some that play, are found;
Here the Albanian proudly treads the ground;
Half whispering there the Greek is heard to prate;
Hark! from the mosque the nightly solemn sound,
The Muezzin's call doth shake the minaret,
"There is no God but God! — to prayer-lo! God is great!"

'Allahu akbar!' affirm the Muslims, and when our bus stopped for a break at the Uji i Ftohtë (Cold Water) springs a ten-minute drive south from Tepelenë, I tried this on an old man with worry beads. 'Bismillahi ar-rahman ar-rahim' he answered fervently but softly, grasping me by both hands. ('In the name of the Compassionate and Merciful God'). A new restaurant below the road sells Albanian chocolate (dark and distinctive) and those rich cakes which turn up as a dessert at most meals. They may be technically beneath Viennese Sachertorte quality, but I enjoyed them, and so did many of the younger members of the party. The transport café at road level is a meeting-point and resting-place for Albanians: foreigners are pointed firmly downhill.

Gjirokastër

Twenty-five minutes after leaving Uji i Ftohtë our coach puffed up the steep slope of Gjirokastër. As it twisted up the zigzag bends we felt like the eagle (*shqipë*) after whom the Albanian (*Shqipëtar*) is said by some scholars to be named. Stuart E. Mann, in *An Albanian Historical Grammar* (1977), regards the derivation of *shqip* as problematic. It may be connected with clear speech (*shqiptoj*=to pronounce; *ha shqip*=to listen to reason; *flas shqip*=to speak Albanian), just as the Greek *barbaroi* ('foreigners') denotes the unclear speech (sounding like 'ba-ba') of the non-Greeks. Mann points out that the word *shqipe* cannot be of Albanian origin, since Indo-European *sk-* produces Albanian *h-*. There is also a word *sqyp* meaning 'beak', likewise of non-Albanian origin.

Gjirokastër is yet another word that does not sound Albanian, and indeed it comes from the Greek Argyrokastron, though the Argyres who built the castle or *kastër* were probably themselves Illyrian. The Ottoman Turks called it Ergeri.

Obviously of Illyrian age, judging by the fortress' foundations, Gjirokastër is a mystery during its earliest centuries. The ancient road system connecting it with Vlorë, Dropull and Lunxhëri, Pogon and Zagori, proves that Gjirokastër must have been a significant site from antiquity, and it is only with the second half of the nineteenth century that the citadel area loses its defensive rôle.

The first mention of Gjirokastër occurs in the chronicle written by I. Kantakouzenos in 1336. Following the Byzantine period, Gjirokastër was controlled by the Zenevishi until the Ottoman conquest of 1417, two years after the establishment of the garrison at Krujë citadel. First Vlorë fell to Ottoman might, then Kaninë, Berat, and Gjirokastër. Sultan Mehmet II decreed that southern Albania was not to become a vassal state, where local princes were permitted to exercise authority under the aegis of the Sublime Porte, but an annexed state in which no Albanian, rich or poor, was to enjoy civil or military powers. The Turks not only created a new administration, but seized all lands, arable and fallow alike, as Turkish property, and it is from the census returns of the years from 1419 that we learn of Gjirokastër's population. In 1431–2, for example, there were 163 dwelling-houses, each probably with an extended family of up to three generations. In 1506–7 there were only 143 houses, but despite the numerous Ottoman incursions and military expeditions, by 1583 there were as many as 434 houses. It was during the seventeenth century that the present conformation of Gjirokastër occurred, its population rising as the rural economy deteriorated and the peasants sought refuge in the towns. Ali Pasha of Tepelenë took the city in 1811, and proceeded to fortify the thirteenth-century castle on its south-western flank. The population, recorded as about 12,000 in 1916, and 10,836 in 1930, is estimated today at about 30,000, including central and surrounding quarters. These quarters lie on three ridges, separated by deep ravines which have given Gjirokastër the euphemistic title of 'City of Two Thousand Steps'. The Albturist Hotel A.Z. Çajupi, on the Çerçiz Topulli Square, is at the foot of the Old Bazaar quarter which will interest most visitors for the huge range of tiny bustling shops in narrow cobbled streets which will remind you of Maltese towns, or Umbrian cities like Todi, Spoleto, or Orvieto. The tourist will also wander with keen eyes over the Pllakë and Hazmurat quarters, for some of the most outstanding private houses. Down in the ravine you may if lucky come across the old Turkish baths which date to the seventeenth century (ask 'Ku është banja?') in the Meçite quarter, not far from the seventeenth-century Meçite Mosque. There is a plan of the baths (fig.37) in Riza's *Qyteti-Muze i Gjirokastrës* (1981), showing that there were five domed rooms beyond the open entrance-area.

The other quarters are Tekke (disclosing a Bektashi interest), Varosh, the open and verdant terrain of Cfakë, the steeply-sloping Manalat and Palorto, and the impressive Dunavat, showing a total mastery of architectural style in the sense of utilising the natural beauty of the

Gjirokastër. Aristocratic houses in the wooded Tekke quarter.

surroundings rather than merely exploiting it. Where Krujë's houses have, like Topsy, just 'growed', and Berat's houses are dominated by the uncomfortable exigencies of river-bed and gorge, by contrast Gjirokastër's urban development has taken account of landforms without being subdued by them. Exuberant, serene, picturesque and ingenious by turns, Gjirokastër evoked in me the same excitement and lightness of heart as San Gimignano and Mistra, in their very different ways. Or say that if Berat and Osum remind you of Toledo and Tajo, then Gjirokastër is the Albanian Ávila. In the clear, fresh mountain air the sun is a benison: men live to a good age, and children prance with a zing in their step.

Your visit will start with the citadel, elongated to defend its ridge on all sides. The retaining walls enclose such a large area that—as can indeed be proved from surviving ruins—many civil buildings were constructed in addition to those vital to the garrison. Nowadays the citadel of

Gjirokastër is devoted to the National Museum of Arms, patriotic statues mingling with arms and ammunition from all periods, with special reference to World War II and the War of National Liberation. In the central hall the young communists of the present day are taught that members of the Albanian Communist Party were the sole liberators of the country from Italian and German domination, and that is indeed how the history books have been rewritten. But the facts are rather more complex.

The Balli Kombëtar consisted of a moderate coalition striving for Albanian independence and the retention of Kosova (in modern Albanian-speaking Yugoslavia) as a part of Albania. To this extent they were more vehemently nationalistic than the communists, who were under the strong influence of Yugoslavia. Like the communists they opposed the Italians, the Germans, and the rule of King Zog. The communists were organized in mobile bands like the Yugoslav partisans, and raided enemy targets mainly from urban refuges, which they changed rapidly to avoid being caught. The Balli Kombëtar recruits, operating in the countryside, were organized according to the familiar pattern of rural peasant rebellions, and were opposed to foreign ideologies such as Marxism, Leninism and Titoism, which occupied the communists in their meetings to the virtual exclusion of the national interest. Indeed, while the liberals and moderate radicals within the Balli Kombëtar failed to provide the strict, harsh leadership that could weld its disparate elements into a forceful military body, the communists decided that they were strong enough to defeat both the Nazis and the Balli Kombëtar, for they had no inclination to share power in post-war Albania.

The civil war fought in 1943–4 is difficult to understand because the losers left few records and the winners changed the record to suit themselves. However, it is possible to piece together some of the evidence to show that the communist partisans fought both royalists and nationalists singly and together, defeating both, and incorporating some nationalist ideology, though discarding the claim to Kosova. The atrocities, numerous on both sides, can be compared with those of the occupying Turks, Italians and Germans at their worst. Allied support, based on pragmatism rather than on principle, came chiefly to the communists, who were thought to have a better chance of defeating the Germans than had either the royalists under Abas Kupi or the nationalists led by Midhat Frashëri. Allied supplies were specifically excluded from use against other Albanians, we learn from E.F. Davies' *Illyrian Venture: the story of the British Military Mission to enemy-occupied Albania, 1943–4* (1952), but Comrade Enver, in his reply to

General Wilson, Supreme Allied Command, Mediterranean Forces, denied that there was a civil war between communists raiding from the south and their rivals entrenched predominantly in the north, and stated that the communists were merely killing Germans and those collaborating with the Germans. It was the concept of 'internal traitors' dating from 1943–4 that allowed later communist propaganda the luxury of asserting that all non-communists were in league with the Germans, though this was certainly not the case.

The United Nations Relief and Rehabilitation Administration put the figures of Albanians killed during World War II at about 30,000, and 100,000 made homeless, as well as about a third of all the country's livestock. When you add to these figures some idea of the roads, bridges, offices and factories put out of action, you will have some idea of the scale of the violence. With a conscious policy of increasing the population, Albania's total of inhabitants even in 1982 is 2.7 million: in 1970 it was 2.1 million; in 1960 1.6, and in 1938 only 1 million.

Mediaeval weapons in glass cases look innocuous enough, but just outside the National Museum of Arms anti-aircraft guns threaten the castle's ancient vaults, gloomy even at mid-day with the perpetual phantom of death prancing above. A U.S.A.F. 'plane is marooned on the

Gjirokastër. Birthplace of Enver Hoxha, now a museum.

battlements, as a forlorn lesson to spies. Where, ask your couriers, does the whitewashed tunnel lead to, below the citadel? In a society dedicated by its masters to pick-axe and rifle, we have seen the pick-axe wielded by dozens at a forced labour camp near Elbasan, or in the Mat valley: this is the shrine of the rifle.

So too is the Museum of National Liberation, open every day from 4 to 7, except on Sundays, 10—12 and 4—9. In the quarter known as Palorto, this is said to have been the house where Comrade Enver was born, but is is clearly unrecognisable, if so, for the magnificent restoration of carved wood ceilings, embroideries, and carpets is very recent. A possibly apocryphal story is told by a visitor who went to see a small house shown as the birthplace of Comrade Enver. The guide explained that it was getting too crowded for all the people who wanted to pay their respects and study in the house-museum, so the Party was going to pull it down and build a much finer birthplace not far away.

Crocodiles of schoolchildren file in quietly for an hour's visit, taking notes in silence as the guide progresses slowly and laboriously from room to room, missing nothing. Some of our party looked carefully at the group photographs for evidence of retouching, and found it. Each phase of the 'National Liberation War' is carefully documented, including the first issue of the communist daily *Zëri i Popullit* and maps to show the gradual extermination of foreigners from Albanian soil. I enjoyed above

Gjirokastër. View into the city centre from the castle.

all the recreation of Gjirokastrian domestic architecture, for apart from the house of the brothers Bajo (1863–1930) and Çerçiz Topulli (1880–1915)—converted into a museum against the Turkish occupation—one cannot view these marvellous houses from within. That is, unless one owns the books of Emin Riza: *Gjirokastra: museum-city* (1978), an album in separate English, Albanian, German, and French editions, and the Albanian-language 349-page monograph *Qyteti-muze i Gjirokastrës* (1981). The main virtue of the former is the series of colour plates in large format, while the latter has hundreds of details in black and white, with plans, drawings and photographs to bring the city to life on the page.

A paradise for students of architecture, Gjirokastër possesses such a variety of forms and structures that a fortnight would suffice only to glimpse a small proportion of them. The great period of house construction extends from about 1800 to about 1860, when many of the possible permutations of design and function were worked out. But the late seventeenth and early eighteenth centuries are represented by fine examples, even if most have been restored. The chief characteristic of the Gjirokastrian house is its graceful solidarity. Whereas cities like Elbasan or Shkodër arose as centres of trade and crafts, Gjirokastër was predominantly a centre of administration and government until the end of the nineteenth century. Wealthy landlords and landowners with estates in Kurvelesh, Lunxhëri and Dropull made Gjirokastër their residence, protecting their extended families in houses of two, three or occasionally even four storeys. Internally, these homes were spacious and elegant and luxuriously furnished. Externally, they resemble the *kullës* of northern Albania in their self-sufficiency for defence, with thick stone walls and tiny windows.

The house is usually compact, with an outer staircase linking the lower two storeys. As in Berat, there is a tendency to use rising terrain as a support for walls and for increasing security: the rocky ridges become an integral part of the builder's plan. This ingenious if natural functionalism is echoed in such interior features as the sitting-room, where niches, shelves, cupboards, window-seats and even divans are carved into the space, instead of jutting out into a plain cube to reduce the overall dimensions as they would in the West (and indeed, in the cheaply-built modern apartment blocks in Albania today). The sitting-room is also distinguished by splendidly intricate wooden carving, wood and stone being the two ingredients common to all houses here. As for the movable furniture, long divans may line as many as three walls, with finely-embroidered throw cushions at intervals along them. One or two low tables may be added for serving coffee to guests. A trunk to hold traditional costumes may sit stolidly in the hall.

Externally, a house is normally plain on all sides but the façade. This may be painted under the protecting broad eaves resting on fine corbels. Again the interplay of wood and stone, of whitewash and colour, of

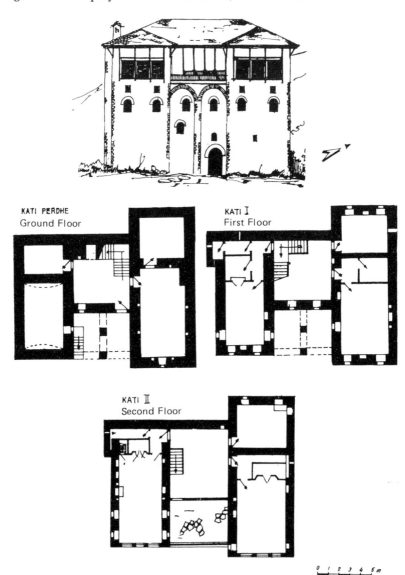

Gjirokastër. Elevation and plan of No.13, Rruga Muhamet Bakiri.

perpendicular and slope all give to the Gjirokastrian houses a collective appearance of strength allied with stark beauty rare in Europe. As a practical guide, I suggest you start house-gazing with the spacious Palorto quarter, since 19 of the 44 houses described in Emin Riza's book are situated there. Seven are in Dunavat, five in Tekke, four in Varosh, three in Manalat, two each in Pllakë and Hazmurat, and one each in Meçite and Cfakë. The example illustrated in plan is no.13, Muhamet Bakiri Street, Palorto.

As tourism is at present strictly limited, the only house you can enter is that of the brothers Topulli, freedom-fighters who led an insurrection against the Turks in 1908. A free-standing mansion recently restored, spotless and shining, it looks anything but a home: nevertheless, in a city whose houses are shut resolutely against suspect strangers it is possible to gain an oblique insight into a society of supremely gifted woodcarvers and stonemasons. Traditionally, many of the southern craftsmen came from Kolonjë and Dangelli regions, from Ersekë to Frashër, but nowadays Gjirokastër produces many of its own craft masters. In 1961 it was declared a museum-city, with a carefully-controlled plan for the protected zone and a less rigid plan for the free zone beyond. Restoration of important houses is a continuous process, as befits the birthplace of Comrade Hoxha, the party secretary.

Ecclesiastical architecture can be divided into two types: the Greek Orthodox churches and the mosques. The earlier of the two extant churches, dated to 1776, is in the Varosh quarter: it was rebuilt in 1833. The second is a three-naved church in the Old Bazaar quarter dating to 1784. The first of two extant mosques, down in the Meçite quarter, was mentioned by the Turkish traveller Evliya Çelebi in the seventeenth century; the second is the Bazaar Mosque of 1757, which is now a theatre. I examined the undisturbed cupola from inside, avoiding the eye of the custodian who was amazed that anyone should want to come up the steps of the theatre and look around several hours before the performance began. Three little children, timidly seeking chewing-gum, smiled up at me from the door. "S'ka!" I replied ("I haven't any") and they giggled into their clenched palms. Down in the crowded bazaar, dark-green Chinese and Soviet lorries were being loaded with refrigerators. A poster advertised a film *Me fal!* ('Excuse me!') at the local cinema. I entered a bookshop and asked politely whether I might pass the wooden barrier and actually browse at the bookshelves instead of gazing from afar. I saw a Greek-language newspaper, which was almost a word-for-word translation of the Albanian-language daily, and made up in strident propaganda what it lacked in news. As well as a crate of volume 36 of the Works of Comrade Enver, I found Shakespeare's *Mbreti Lir*

(*King Lear*), and Albanian translations from the Venezuelan Rómulo Gallegos and the Italian Carlo Levi. Then to the foot of the hill, where new apartment blocks five to seven storeys high built to rather poor specifications for the masses contrast with the aristocratic single-family residences of earlier days on the commanding ridges. A desultory game of football was being played on the uneven Subi Bakiri pitch.

And how do the people of Gjirokastër live today? It has a Higher Teachers' Training College, reflecting the fact that, with Korçë, it is the old stronghold of the intellectual class largely driven into exile after World War II, when Islamic and Christian religious leaders were turned out of their institutions and compelled to perform manual tasks in field and factory; when artists and thinkers, writers and composers, were given the stark choice between conforming to the party line or clearing out.

Gjirokastër is also famous for cheese, yoghurt, and the famous local dish *hoshaf* (served to tourists in the Hotel Çajupi) consisting of junket and figs. Factories are dedicated to tobacco, cigarettes, chemicals, shoes, and leather. I am afraid my bias is showing: I love Gjirokastër dearly, and suggest that no visit to Albania could ever be complete without adequate time spent here, largely on your own, far from fellow-tourists or helpful, observant guides. The fireflies at night are as evocative of the Middle Ages and its superstitions as the narrow cobbled streets and occasional disembodied laughter from behind a stone wall.

Gjirokastër's hotel, the Çajupi, is so-called in honour of the pen-name of the poet Andon Z. Çako (1866–1930), who was born in a village near Gjirokastër and, like the folklorists Spiro Dine and Thimi Mitko, left Albania for Egypt. He became a successful lawyer in his adopted land, but he is now best known for his translations from La Fontaine's *Fables*, and for his nostalgic and patriotic verse. Here is the title-poem from his book *Father Tomori* (1902), translated with the kind assistance of Albturist's Flora and Lejla over Turkish coffee in the Hotel Çajupi.

> Father Tomor, I am crying:
> Learn what it means to be Albanians.
> They have been praised for their courage,
> And in battle they have been triumphant.
> Vendetta, religion, have not sundered Albanians.
> Passing their lives with rifle at the ready
> They love their homeland and will not forsake it.
> All Albania has flowered, and the people are free.
> Men and women love their country;
> Boys and girls still sing of liberty.
> How is Albania now? Suffering under the Turkish sway.

Albanians, governed like a flock of sheep,
Go unshod, unclothed, and die of hunger.
Albanians—but today there *are* no Albanians!
Turks and Greeks divide us.
Priest and imam, church and mosque deceive us.
Albania is shattered.
Father Tomor, beloved mountain, you know
What has happened, what befell,
You know and I don't need to tell you,
But you tell me what will now befall
Helpless Albania, listen to Father Tomor!
Your country makes no progress!
Faith has divided you, so don't believe in God,
For faiths have no place. You Christians, you Muslims
Are of the same blood. You poor people, born
In the same land, you are all Albanians,
Neither Greeks nor Turks.
Get rid of this danger! Beware of the foe!
The traitors! The evil!
Unite and swear a truce
In memory of Skënderbeg
To cherish our homeland
And not let it fall low.
Arise and save it yourselves!
Don't count on the Turks!
Don't trust in the Greeks!
But cherish your homeland.
The day has come to fight
For free Albania —
To die or survive
Like men of valour.

5
Sarandë and Butrint

If the whole of southern Albania is a Victorian landscape-painter's vision of Paradise, many would nevertheless argue that the stretch between Gjirokastër and Sarandë, over the Muzina Pass, offers that tremendous surge of emotion which a Frenchman will feel on first encountering Gustave Doré's illustrations to Dante, or an Englishman on coming face to face with the staggering visual imagination of John Martin. William Beckford satirised in *Biographical Memoirs of Extraordinary Painters* (1780) the eighteenth-century artists who sought to express the stupendous in wild moors and craggy mountainsides, with crashing waterfalls and startling ravines. But this is no more than minimal art in the Albanian context. And though one may be timorously overawed in the Himalayas, or even in the Alps, distances in Albania are so relatively short that a whole day's landscapes can be comprehended with one wide sweep of the mental camera.

Driving out of Gjirokastër southward, one passes Sofratike and other Greek villages on hill slopes to the right of the road, and then in a few minutes there is Glina: the village where the staple mineral water is bottled. At Gjorgucat crossroads a left turn would take you to Kakavi and over the Greek border, but at present the border is closed to tourists. Greek irredentism is a constant fear of the Albanian authorities, despite recent reassurances from the Greek Government that 'Northern Epiros' (as the irredentists call southernmost Albania) is not claimed for Greece. We turn right at Gjorgucat, climbing up to the Muzina Pass, where Muzina's abandoned village (all but the church) had been burnt down by the Nazis.

The highest point of the Pass is 650m. above sea level, and is 23km. beyond Gjorgucat and 21km. from Sarandë. Olives and chestnut trees thrive in this clime. Then we emerge into full view of the Bistricë 2 Hydro-electric Station, quickly followed by the Stalin Hydro-electric Station. At last I recognised the poetic impulse that fired Evgeni Evtushenko to create his long poem 'The Bratsk Hydro-Electric Station', in fact not the simple eulogy that its title might suggest, but a wide-

Dropull Valley, south of Gjirokastër. A Greek-minority village, from the road to Sarandë.

ranging philosophical epic consisting of apparently disparate scenes from the execution of Stepan Razin to the 20th Party Congress, the whole informed with an urgent socialist message which the poet dominates by the force of his imagery and the boldness of his undertaking.

If American poetry achieves truth by a process of careful checks and balances (Eliot, Lowell) or by radiant individualism (Whitman, Emily Dickinson, Berryman), then the best of Communist poetry (Mayakovsky, Evtushenko) is stirred by the collective ideal, by construction and reconstruction, and by transformation of the land. Of course a great many penalties have to be paid for rapid development, and Albania's cautious development in all fields has been interrupted by political feuds which are of Albania's own making (according to her critics) or caused by internal and external saboteurs (to adopt the local view). The latter theory is weakened by the Soviet Government's writing off in 1957 debts worth US$105 million accumulated over 1949–57. The hydro-electric stations in the north (Vaut të Dejës and Drita e Partisë), in the centre (Engels, Karl Marks [sic], and Lenin), and these two in the south have enabled Albania to export electricity: 850 million kWh to Yugoslavia annually, and more to other countries via the Yugoslav network.

Just before the crossroads to Sarandë (11km.) and to Delvinë (9km.) the Church of Mesopotamos can be seen across fields to the left. And it was here that relations with our Albturist couriers reached their ebb. 'We may not stop here!' stated Flora, as one or two asked permission to stop and take photographs of the monastery and church constructed by order of Constantine IX (1042–54). With rebellion floating throughout the bus, Flora finally allowed us to get out to look at the church from afar. Seven adventurous spirits, realising that the church was close and we were already very near our day's destination, forded the stream and headed in a straggle of defiance, recriminations sounding in our ears. Like Lot's wife, we turned back to look, yet somehow remained unsalificated. At the barbed-wire fence protecting the sacred building from being worshipped in, or even being examined internally, we were accosted by an old shepherd with strict instructions to let nobody pass. I interpreted his 'You can't get in here without a telegram from the Ministry', upon which a redoubtable lady from Kensington presented her bearer's pass to the Chelsea Flower Show. 'Will this do?' she asked, as someone else hopefully produced an international driving licence, and a third showed his reader's card to Newcastle University Library.

Sarandë. Waterfront.

As the photographers clicked away, I patted a stolid pregnant donkey and perused Aleksandër Meksi's article 'Kisha e Mesopotamit' in volume 1 of *Monumente të Kulturës në Shqipëri* (1975). Four of the five plates in the article are of the interior, which is all I shall ever see of it, for we were prohibited from entering by the shepherd, and trailed back, across a field of shattered gravestones that looked as though it had been the victim of a demolition squad. The only untouched marble gravestone, surrounded by railings, was inscribed 'Thoma Kristo Kuçuqi, 1913–1980 Kujtim nga familja' (Remembered by his family). Our driver and couriers were infuriated with us on our return: 'You must not go anywhere without our permission' (though both earlier and later we wandered freely enough); 'When I say you must not visit a church, then you must believe me'; 'There, you see there is no key'; 'If you ask in advance, we can arrange something' (though the programme was never fixed more than one day ahead at a time and had to be cleared with Albturist in Tirana each evening by telephone); 'You English have no idea of obedience'; 'You are very rude, and you do not apologise'.

Our recalcitrance led to divisions within the group: the majority felt we should do exactly as we were told; the minority felt we had a right to have our preferences consulted before the next day's itinerary was settled, and again when we discovered special events in the town where we were to spend the night. The couriers imposed their will on the silent majority, and consulted the wishes of the vocal minority, throughout the rest of the trip.

Sarandë

We arrived in Sarandë at 12.10, and found our rooms in the Hotel Butrinti. Whereas Room 27 at Gjirokastër Hotel Çajupi had been tiny, with a washbasin, locked communal shower and two locked communal toilets, Room 315 in Sarandë's Hotel Butrinti was comparatively large, with a private basin, shower and toilet. Our first glimpse of Corfu from Albania was from our side-verandah: we heard a voice on the verandah below 'What do you say we make a run for Corfu!' and muffled laughter at the joke. The Butrinti is the only modern hotel in Sarandë, set among prickly pears, oleanders and hydrangeas, with piles of logs below us to the side, heaps of coal at the back, and before us the Strait of Corfu dividing capitalist Corfu from communist Albania. 'Don't ask at the reception for a bedroom', warned a sign in Albanian, 'because they are all occupied'. All the year round, by foreign tourists. Our lunch was satisfactory: risotto with a plate of olives, veal with salad and chips, a slice of rich cake, and fresh peaches.

Sarandë is the Albanian form of the Greek *saranta*, 'forty', from *Agii*

Sarandë. *Rrojtore* (Barber's) and *Rrobaqepesi burra + gra* (Men's and Women's Tailor).

Saranta, 'Forty Saints', the name of a Byzantine monastery. In classical times it was Onchesmos, appearing briefly as Cicero, returning from the East, reported a favourable wind from Onchesmos. Then it fell into obscurity in Ottoman times, achieving a brief recovery when Ali Pasha of Tepelenë used it as a port for Yannina. The Greeks made Sarandë a base for their advance into Albania in 1940. Its population has risen from 1,000 in 1926 to about 8,800 today. Sarandë skirts a bay about 1¼km. wide by nearly 1km., deep, thirty fathoms deep half a mile from the coast and ten fathoms at a thousand feet from the shore. The town is protected from all but south-west winds by the Eremecë range of low mountains. Modern Sarandë dates from the 1950s: and its appearance is clean, neat, and somehow reminiscent of a tiny well-kept Greek port.

I sought ancient Onchesmos, and found opposite a tourist shop set back one street from the promenade some impressive excavations, open to the public on three sides, without attendants, the fourth side being barred surrealistically by a metal gate. Don't bother with the gate. I avoided buying a glazed ceramic eagle and a glass flamingo in the tourist shop, where a lady was patiently knitting a garment that looked like a giant's pullover.

A few columns have been re-erected, but the most interesting survivals from Onchesmos, the port of the once-flourishing city of Phoinike (now

Finiq, a few km. inland), are the mosaics, both geometric and figurative, such as a splendid peacock. Hoping to buy a political poster, I was advised by a journalist on the local paper to try the Post Office, open 7–12 and 4–7. At ten past four the Post Office opened but the staff were bewildered by any suggestion that they might stock posters for sale. I found a good bookshop, where I bought the *Trésor du chansonnier populaire albanais* (1975) published by the Folklore Institute of the Academy of Sciences. Over an ice-cream at an *akullore* I eagerly devoured this marvellous compendium which is divided into folksongs of nature, lullabies, love songs, wedding songs, ballads, and historical epics, with pp.263–325 devoted to the War of National Liberation and propaganda for socialism and the Party of Labour in particular. A specimen of the latter is 'O Party of Great Renown':

> O Party of Great Renown,
> That warning to those vultures,
> To those Greeks and Serbs,
> To the United States Sixth Fleet
> That blow to the cunning,
> Whose mask you have lifted.
> Long live the Party,
> Our Army, and Albania!

Contrasting with the above, here is a love song from Tropojë in northeast Albania, very near the Yugoslav border:

> *Love You Never Forget*
> Under the shade of the cherry-tree,
> Bardhe stays to weep
> And her tears which fall
> She tries to dry with the corner of her shawl.
>
> But poor Bardhe cries and cries
> And the wood absorbs the damp:
> Begins to mould and mildew.
>
> Her heart full, her throat constricted,
> She tells her plaint,
> Cursing winter pastures,
> Cursing summer pastures,
> The house, the shepherds:
>
> > 'O shepherds, may you be dishonoured,
> > May the flower never bloom,
> > May those mountains crack,
> > May Valbonë river nevermore
> > Water your valley.'

> He hears her, on the peak above,
> Zane, Zane, who anxiously calls:
>   'My sister, my sister, why do you weep?
>   Why, I know nothing, O why?'
>
> Little Bardhe stays to weep
> Under the shade of the cherry-tree,
> But why I cannot tell.
>   'Little Bardhe cries for a boy
>   She has not seen so long.
>   When will he come again to see her?
>   A heart dries too, and turns to ash.
>   Stone shatters, and turns to grit.
>   But love you never forget.'

An evening stroll under the waving palms of Sarandë's neat promenade illuminated at night: the coaster called *Lezhë* was moving off its berth at the northern end of the bay. A shop-sign read 'Hapet nga ora gjashtë gjë më nentë' (Open from six o'clock until nine), but the shop was already locked at 7.30.

Weaving up and down the steps of Sarandë's three roads terraced around the curving bay like any hillside in Albania, I recalled my honeymoon and the much steeper stairways of stony Valletta. But just as Malta is the colour of sandy Arabia's Empty Quarter, lowland Albania is the hue of Ireland's hills and valleys. 'Bujqesia çestjë e të gjithë popullit', hammer the huge red hoardings: 'Agriculture is the concern of the whole people.'

The *passeggiata* entices most families out into the warm dusk, some with arms linked, a few chatting, but most taking mental notes, calculating... You could be in a drably-dressed, carless, wartime Taranto.

Now the amblers gradually drifted away into bars, restaurants, and sitting-rooms, like sand into caverns before evening gusts. I stood, human obelisk, on the darkling beach, trying to admit serenity into my mind crowded with the day's impressions. If only thinking could be swept under the waves and we could be left for a moment thoughtless: in a band of silence, as if on a revolving turntable with the volume of confusions turned so low as to be inaudible... But even a narrow, empty spit of beach on a jet-black night is a mob of fossil shells ground to minute grains of sand; waves roar rampant farther or nearer according to your venturing—sibilant as if they had begun learning to speak with the letter S, reached confident SH, and then drowned their mentor.

Sarandë. Street scene. ▷

Butrint

If you need to change money at Sarandë, remember to ask for your passport at the hotel desk before seeking the bank in the town centre (ten minutes' walk): you will find it open from 7.30–11.30 a.m. The old typewriters may be of pre-World War II vintage, but the calculators and other equipment must be more recently imported from Italy or Yugoslavia. Our bus to Butrint started at 9.25; on the way we admired a fine sunflower crop and wheat grown by the shores of the Bistricë river and by Lake Butrint. In 16km. we arrived at Butrint, the Greek Buthroton and Roman Buthrotum. There is a magnificent view across the Lake of Butrint (classical Lake of Pelos), about 3.5km. from the sea, and fine conditions to observe sea and marsh birds, including duck, woodcock and snipe.

The most obvious signs of fortification from afar are Ali Pasha's lakeside watch-tower, a defensive tower on the seaward side, and the remains of a wall, protecting the hill of Butrint from attack by sea. But don't imagine that Butrint achieved prominence for the first time in the eighteenth century: the Chaones, a southern Illyrian tribe, had fortified the rock towards the beginning of the first millennium B.C.; they in turn succeeded a Stone Age people attested by recent excavations. Greek colonists took over from the Illyrians—or more probably lived in uneasy proximity with them—in the sixth century B.C., and by good fortune the great orator Cicero has left us some details on Roman Buthrotum, when the town minted its own coins, and enjoyed security for a time, and at a price. It was the seat of a Byzantine bishop in the tenth century, but fell to the Normans in the eleventh, to the Hohenstaufens in the thirteenth, and to the Venetians in the fourteenth.

J.C. Hobhouse, friend of Byron, wrote in 1813: 'Butrinto (near which, if we may credit Pouqueville, are to be seen some remains of the 'lofty' city of Buthrotum), was so long in the possession of the Venetians, that the inhabitants of the town and neighbourhood are, for the most part, Christians of the Latin Church; and there is a Roman Catholic Bishop established in the place, who is equally protected by his present master, Ali, as he was by the French.' And it is still the eighteenth-century citadel of Ali Pasha Tepelenë that grips the imagination today: his elegant towers look like hides for royal hunters and fishers—one could imagine the Albrecht of *Giselle* here, or perhaps the Actaeon of Titian's *Diana and Actaeon*.

The excavations of Butrint were carried on by an Italian team led by Luigi Ugolini during the decade from 1928: the Albanians bitterly accuse the Italian team of having taken away objects from the museum and from the excavations. However, it is not unusual for archaeological

Butrint. Ferry.

expeditions to be granted the right to take home with them certain examples or specimens of finds they have made, and it is by no means certain that the Italians exceeded their contractual demands. It is, however, certain that no Albanian was then qualified to excavate, and even now, as a result of restrictions on travel, study, and book and journal acquisition, one can see that very little has been done to add to the finds due to Ugolini and his colleagues.

The plan of Buthroton can best be understood by ascending the hill where the museum is situated. There you can identify the acropolis wall founded in the eighth century B.C. and rebuilt in the fourteenth century A.D.; a lower wall nearly a kilometre long; and a third protective wall on the other side of the canal.

An official visit, shepherded by the young guide Rasim, begins at the largest baths complex—the City Baths, with some fine geometric mosaics in black and white in the frigidarium. Next is the theatre, very small for a city of such importance, with only nineteen rows of seats so far exposed in the *cavea*, of which the first and most elegant was dedicated to the city dignitaries. The western *parodos* bears inscriptions proving that the theatre was built in the fourth century B.C. with revenue from the neighbouring Temple of Asklepios or Aesculapius. The *orchestra* and *scaena* of the theatre are reconstructions of recent date. The Temple of

Butrint. Roman theatre from above.

Butrint. Mosaic in the baptistery.

Butrint. Basilica.

the Greek god of healing, who was dexterously borrowed into the Roman pantheon, consists of a covered narthex and modest room dating to the second century A.D. on earlier foundations. The theatre pool stirred to reveal lazy terrapins, cautious frogs, and water-snakes unwinding as if to music. The sound of cicadas and the dance of dragonflies numbed the senses with that Mediterranean enchantment which overcomes the traveller on Delos, and at Rhodian Lindos. One expects centaurs, dryads, and mischievous *amorini* to emerge from behind Greek columns. This is the weather for an *après-midi d'un faune*; these are the mysterious moods of Poussin's classicism with the colours of Cézanne's or Picasso's Provence. We wander among the private houses of Roman Butrint using the imagination which we may not employ in the factual surroundings of time-pinned Pompeii and Herculaneum: here are the remnants of a house with a peristyle, there the figments of a shop. The imposing baptistery still possesses its mosaics, but they are dry, stifled under gravel, not generously spread with water to bring out their rich light and colour. Nobody makes the comparison between the expansive Roman empire and the introspective Albanian rural state.

The gravel on the floor of the baptistery conceals seven concentric circles of polychrome mosaics, five of them with geometric and vegetable motifs, the remaining two with sixty-four roundels showing birds and animals. I cleared away the gravel to reveal a dog in one roundel and a cockerel in another, both against plain white backgrounds. Some motifs were replaced by Christian symbols when the building was turned into a baptistery in the sixth century A.D.

You will come across a nymphaeum of the second century A.D. The statues of Apollo and Dionysos have been removed from the nymphaeum for some reason—probably connected with security—to the museum on the hill. Snakes glide silently by, wild grass moving to indicate their passage. Now you enter a basilica of the fourteenth century (again beware of snakes!) with an apse and three naves. Close by are the walls of the lower town dated to the fourth century B.C., with an easily-defensible gate (Porta Skea) denying access from the water. Now examine the lower city walls: their monumental strength and power, virtually impervious to any attack but treason. We followed the walls as far as the Gate of the Lion and Bull, then doubled back to the third-century A.D. well, and climbed the hill to the museum. A head of Zeus, Greek inscriptions, a copy of the superb Aphrodite of the fourth century B.C. (the original being in Tirana): these are some of the highlights of the small museum. But I preferred the landscape and seascape from the citadel terrace, with its toylike cannon and battlements. The afternoon had been polished by the sun to the radiance of a gold coin freshly minted. While photographers snapped at boats in the reeds, and at grey granite columns slanting to compromise between their original vertical and their ultimate horizontal, I closed my eyes and let a butterfly hover above an oleander: is the butterfly dreaming Butrint, or is Butrint dreaming the butterfly?

Ksamil

The State Farm of Ksamil has 1,500 inhabitants, and it was there that we took lunch, for there is no hotel, restaurant or even café at Butrint (carry a bottle of mineral water against the heat). Risotto and salad was followed by a whole fresh fish and chips, rich cake and cherries. Albanian hospitality is like this: generous and unquestioning, very like the welcome given by the Chinese.

At lunch an anecdote was told of a Turk, during Ottoman times, who was about to shoot an Albanian rebel. The rebel seemed completely calm and resigned, impelling the Turk to ask if he had ever been in a worse situation. 'Yes,' responded the Albanian at once, 'when a guest arrived and I had not even a crust of bread to offer him.' It is said that the Turk let the rebel go, which says as much for Turkish generosity as for Albanian hospitality.

While the remainder of the group relaxed or swam in the sparkling sea

Ksamil State Farm. View down to the beach and rocks.

below the rest-house, I ambled down into Ksamil village. Hot bitumen was oozing blackly on the surface of the road, so I walked beside it to keep my sandals clean. On the village notice-board the names of outstanding workers were pinned up, with their achievements spelt out for general emulation:

1st Brigade, under Brigadier Vasillo Braçka, 1981, fruit production exceeded plan target by 137%.

7th Brigade, under Brigadier Filip Papa, 1981, fruit production exceeded plan target by 138%.

Experimental Brigade, under Brigadier Sotir Dafillo, 1981, fruit production exceeded plan target by 155%.

2nd Brigade, under Brigadier Jani Shanë, 1981, exceeded plan target by 139%. I discussed the orange crop with a few workers still not taking their siesta—'It will be ready in November, December and January,' they said. I talked to a bachelor called Lazam, but he would not allow himself to be photographed.

The party simmered in frustration at the long delay before a farm representative would come and talk to us, but this is southern Europe, where time is servant not master: the homely Yorkshire philosophy of 'there's all tomorrow not touched yet' shook hands across the seas with Indonesian *jam karet* (rubber time) precisely here in Ksamil. At length the formality of lecturing in Albanian and interpreting into English began, with the usual statistics compared as a percentage with 1938 figures, and not with recent production quantities.

It is impressive that so much of once-barren hillside is now reclaimed for fruit trees—olives and citrus fruit—but the enormous expenditure of human energy made me wince. The United States, employing 5% of its work-force in agriculture, can not only feed 100% of its population, but also export grain in massive quantities to the inefficient, bureaucratic, collectivised Soviet Union. And Albanian agriculture is decades behind that of the Soviet Union in management and mechanisation... The farmworkers here start at 7 a.m., and work eight hours a day six days a week, with fifteen days off a year—conditions that would make Western farmworkers rise in rebellion, or at least struggle for an independent trade union to represent them.

Ksamil has its own new Palace of Culture, and it looks strangely abandoned, like a Taj Mahal on the moon. Can we see the library? No, it is locked. Can we see the theatre? No, it is locked. Can we see the cinema, the bar...? No, they are all locked. And nobody at all can be found to open them, my dears. Where now are the graves of Ksamil—its past? No, there is no past, but only a present and a future, for Ksamil is where young people are sent: *qytet pa varreza*—a city without graves. They are the soldiers of farming, each brigade of young men and women led by a brigadier who shall fulfil his work plan. At the end of the day they can read the party newspaper or listen to the Government on the radio. Without foreign news, foreign books, or the possibilities of travel, they are evading the rest of the twentieth century like flies in a locked room. As our coach back to Sarandë was filled with charming folk-music on Tiranafonia cassette tapes, the penalties for criminality were explained by Lejla of Albturist over the microphone: 'Seven years in prison for a thief, 25 years in prison for a murderer followed by hard labour, Albanian traitors are shot, and foreign traitors are taken before a People's Court.'

'And what happens to them if they are convicted, Lejla?'

'Tomorrow we leave Sarandë at nine a.m.'

At three a.m. I woke to a scream in a room nearby, overlooking the harbour. 'It was the searchlight in the harbour which blinded me as I turned over and opened my eyes,' said a woman at breakfast. 'It reminded me of the War.'

What reminded *me* of the War was the view of Corfu and the channel in which two British ships were badly damaged by mines in 1946, with the loss of forty-four lives. Albania refused to indemnify Britain, claiming that whoever had laid the mines (probably the Yugoslavs), it was not Albania. Britain took the case to the International Court of

Justice at The Hague, and was awarded £900,000 in 1949 on the grounds that Albania had been responsible for the safe passage of ships along an international shipping lane in her territorial waters.

Albania in turn demands the return of gold, now estimated to be worth more than US$26.5 million, seized by the Allies from the Germans at the end of World War II. The gold lies in the vaults of the Bank of England, nominally on behalf of the Tripartite Commission for the Restitution of Monetary Gold. Claims are made on Albania's gold by the U.S.A. and Italy, while Britain insists on retaining that portion corresponding to the Corfu Channel Award. Albania rejects not only the British claim, but also those of Italy and the U.S.A. The United States Government requires compensation for property nationalised by the Communist regime, and a powerful exile lobby in Washington has prevented a settlement. Since Albania is the only European state with which Britain has no diplomatic relations, it was suggested by a leader-writer in *The Times*, 19 March 1981, that Britain should take the initiative in offering Albania the greater part of the gold, retaining with Albanian agreement minor sums, with prior Italian and American approval, for the settlement of all outstanding claims. *The Times* adds: 'Britain should now pursue this [policy] with more energy, flexibility and generosity than it has shown so far'.

Albania's communist regime has always been suspicious of the U.K. and U.S.A., frequently without reason. However, we now know that Anglo-American subversion was attempted in the Spring of 1951; first by parachutists dropped in the north of the country, then by other groups infiltrating by land, sea and air. The whole operation failed spectacularly, because the British Secret Intelligence operation was betrayed by the Soviet agent Kim Philby (see *My Secret War*, 1968). All the agents were efficiently intercepted and executed, and the exercise (as far as we know) never repeated until a landing force was 'liquidated', to use the official terminology, on the coast in September 1982.

6
Krujë and Elbasan

The way up from the plain at Fushë-Krujë to the mountain stronghold of Krujë is in some sense a journey from our time to the age of Gjergj Kastrioti Skënderbeg (1405–68), the national hero of Albania, who is constantly compared explicitly and implicitly with the present leader Comrade Enver Hoxha.

Krujë

You come into Krujë past age-old olive trees and lime-kilns, with limestone outcrops offering the barest grazing to a few sheep and goats. Then shrubs and oaks replace the olives, and finally the conifers take over. 'Krujë' means 'spring', and of course there is no shortage of fresh water at these cool heights. The air invigorates you after the hot, humid plain of Tirana, and one can easily imagine why the old Illyrian settlement of Zgërdhesh was abandoned in the fourth century, and the refugees from the hotter, more exposed foothills chose to defend a mountain eyrie instead.

We first find a mention of Krujë in ecclesiastical records of the ninth century, as a bishop's see. The Byzantines held the city up to c.1190, when the first Albanian feudal state was declared at Krujë under the archon Progon (1190–8), who ruled a principality covering almost half of northern Albania but excluding the cities of the plains. The Serb, Stefan Nemanja, took Dukagjin from the state of Arbania, so that its limits were now the rivers Drin and Shkumbin. Arbania survived throughout the rule of Progon's sons Gjin (1198–1206) and Demetrios (1206–16), but in 1216 it fell under the sway of Epiros, in 1230 under the Bulgarians, and in 1240 again under Epiros. Autonomy became so tenuous that it was soon no longer worthy of the name. Foreign invaders continue to fight over the dying body of a torn and bleeding Albania until an Ottoman garrison was permanently stationed at Krujë in 1415, and thence others quickly spread to the rest of the country.

The youngest of Gjon Kastrioti's four sons, Gjergj, was sent with his three brothers as a hostage to the Sultan at Constantinople in 1415. In the capital—again in the view of his first biographer Barlezio—he converted to Islam and impressed his tutors at the military school for pages, later adding to his Islamic name Iskandar (Albanian *Skënder*) the honorific title *beg* for valour on the field of battle. Then in 1443 he suddenly left the Ottoman army fighting Hunyadi, the Hungarian hero, and returned to Albania. Could his heart have been inflamed by the independent stance of Hunyadi, provoking a similar hunger for national integrity? A homesickness with its own radical cure? We cannot tell, for Barlezio's saga has been impugned by Fan Noli and others, and it is just as likely that Gjergj was appointed vali of the areas (Jonima, Misia, and Skuria) later subsumed under the *vilayet* of Krujë, called by the Turks Akce Hisar (White Castle). Nominally, a vassal of the Sultan, Gjergj began to plot for a free Albania, first with Venice, then with Ragusa (now Dubrovnik), with Alfonso V of Naples, and with Vladislas of Hungary, trying all potential allies in a bid to wrest power from the Porte. Hunyadi's rebellion of 1442 against the Turks began with such success that the Pope quickly persuaded other Balkan leaders to rise against Islam and the Turks. As the Turks retreated near Niš on 3 November 1443, Gjergj withdrew his nephew Hamza and 300 Albanian horsemen and headed for Dibër and then Krujë, seizing the latter with a forged *firman* from the Sultan followed by a surprise night attack to massacre the Turkish garrison. It was hardly to be expected that the might of the Turks would shrivel under this one defeat, and indeed they sent onslaught after ineffective onslaught on Skënderbeg and his castle of Krujë, year after year, until the time of reckoning came.

It seems hardly conceivable that Krujë's sleepy citadel above the wide green plain should have been the scene of one of Europe's most titanic struggles, but in May 1450 the Ottoman Sultan Murad II set out from Constantinople with a hundred thousand men to crush once and for all the Albanian army which had been united since 1444 by Skënderbeg's personal recruiting campaign. He aimed to storm the citadel of Krujë and to hold the Albanian countryside with Krujë as his capital. Skënderbeg's personal magnetism ensured that all those Albanians fit to take up arms were armed and ready for combat, a total of 17,500 at the most, who were thus outnumbered by five to one. Skënderbeg divided his peasant troops into three bands. Fifteen hundred led by Count Uran were provisioned to withstand the siege within the citadel itself. The two major forces of 8,000 each were split up, the first under Skënderbeg to harry the rear of the Ottoman army once it had encamped below Krujë, and the other forming small bands of *guerrilleros* to ambush, raid, and snipe at the Turkish caravan on its cumbersome trail from Macedonia. Murad II, despite casualties suffered *en route*, reached Krujë on 14 May

1450 and immediately ordered the besieged troops to surrender. Count Uran refused, and with the Ottoman lines cut off by Skënderbeg, some of whose mobile units had now rejoined the Albanian rearguard, the Sultan ordered the bombardment of the citadel which he 'had hoped to secure intact. The Albanians were thus secure within the citadel, brilliantly successful in *guerrilla* warfare before, and triumphant in intercepting supplies sent for the siege army first from Macedonia, and later from Venice.

Since Murad II realised that his troops would mutiny if ordered to withstand the hostile winter encamped in a trap below Krujë, after four and a half months he retreated with losses estimated at more than twenty thousand—that is exceeding the strength of the whole Albanian army. Ragusa congratulated Skënderbeg, 'magnificus et potens' on his stupendous victory.

But such fairy tales have a way of ending happily never after, and despite another victory for Skënderbeg at Krujë in 1467, the resistance crumbled after his death from fever the following year, leaving only Lek Dukagjin to continue the struggle against Turkey, with valuable help from Venice. Predictably, with most of the Albanian nobles fled abroad or gone over to the enemy, Krujë definitively fell to Sultan Mehmet on 16 June 1478. The Venetians signed a peace treaty with Turkey in the following January, taking Durrës, Ulcinj and Antivari for themselves and ceding Shkodër, Lezhë, Drisht, Himarë and Sopot to the Turks.

Rebellions sparked off in one town here and another village there, year after year, but the cohesive force of a national leader was absent, and the Ottoman government played the 'divide and rule' game so successfully that to all intents and purposes opposition virtually ceased in 1606. Wars and sieges had decimated towns, razed hill villages, almost eliminated livestock, and damaged crops. To escape crippling taxes and the danger of massacre, thousands sought refuge with the allied Kingdom of Naples, which included Calabria and Sicily. There they did not so much intermarry (after all their language and history were remote from those of their hosts) as establish new 'Arbëresh' villages—about a hundred of them—where Albanian was spoken, written, and even taught in schools.

For the British military strategist Wolfe, Skënderbeg surpassed 'all captains, both ancient and modern, in his ability to lead a small defensive army'. He also combined skill in directing *guerrilla* warfare on the small scale with large-scale political alliances which kept the Ottoman Empire at bay over a period of decades, and for many years at desperation point. But can we assess his premature aspiration to Albanian statehood as sensible, cautious, or even wise? If politics is the art of the possible, Skënderbeg was not a politician but a visionary, a

Don Quixote rather than a Ho Chi Minh. For whereas the skilled and united *guerrilleros* of the Vietcong won their war of attrition against the vastly superior forces of the French and then the United States, there can be no argument with the position that Skënderbeg delayed a Turkish victory, but quite certainly lost in the end, and at a price which future centuries would rue. Krujë, like the equally prosperous cities of Berat, Durrës and Shkodër, was so ravaged by massacre, plague, and famine, that it has not recovered even to this day: there were 4,835 inhabitants in 1930, 4,500 in 1938, and 6,000 in 1969. The people became Muslim, some by conviction, and some because the taxes inflicted on non-Muslims were so high (45 aspres in the fifteenth century to 305 in the early seventeenth and 780 in the mid-seventeenth, for some grades of taxpayer, to give a rough comparison) that most people turned for submission to Islam simply in order to survive.

The tale of Skënderbeg has become familiar in epic poetry (Fan Noli) history, biography, drama (E. Koliqi), music and the remarkable novel by Ismail Kadare *Kështjella* (1970), translated into many languages including English (*The Castle*, Tirana, 1974; reprinted in 1980 by Gamma Publishing Company, P.O. Box 206, New York, N.Y. 10008). Kadare is something of an enigma, for despite being the most distinguished writer of modern Albania, often rising above the crude official party propaganda, he is chief editor of *Les Lettres Albanaises* and member of the Writers' Union which enforces the propaganda. Born in Gjirokastër in 1936, Kadare studied literature at Tirana University, and at the Gorki Institute in Moscow up to 1960. He lives in Tirana with his wife Elena, the first Albanian woman novelist. He began writing lyric verse, publishing eight such collections from 1954 to 1978, but made his name internationally in 1964 with the novel translated into English as *The General of the Dead Army*, a work resonant with regret and irony, while a reviewer in *Le Figaro* compared the French version of Kadare's *The Great Winter* (1974–7) with Tolstoy's *War and Peace*. Kadare has taken up invitations to visit China, Sweden and France, and I met him briefly at the German-Albanian Friendship Society in Frankfurt in October 1981.

The castle of Kadare's novel is elliptical, with a perimeter of some 800m. following almost exactly the contours of the isolated peak. Although battles and sieges have damaged and even utterly destroyed parts of the great inhabited citadel, certain elements remain to beckon the imagination back in time. As you enter the citadel from the path below, a totally reconstructed historical museum dominates the gateway, replacing in 1982 the old museum named for Skënderbeg. You are now at the northern point of the citadel, with the clock tower at the

Krujë. New museum of Skënderbeg at the crest of the citadel, from the Clock Tower.

north-east, the highest point. It is said that this was the *campanile* of Skënderbeg's own church, and the bell tolled almost as often to warn of enemy attacks as to summon worshippers to prayer. Near this tower, on the bare rockface, fires would be lit to communicate with *guerrilla* forces operating as skirmishers in the valleys below and on distant hillsides. As for the provision of water, a cistern for storing rainwater has been found just by the northern entrance, while the Taslloi springs (once defended by secondary walls protecting them for the castle dwellers) can still be seen by clambering down a path at the south-west walls. After the Ottomans took their dearly-won castle of Krujë, they rebuilt the walls on the northern side, with openings for firearms, to make Krujë as impregnable against the Albanians as it had been impregnable against themselves. The earthquake of 1617 caused the cracking and collapse of many hill structures, including the citadel, but in 1832, on the Sultan's orders, the Albanian feudal castles were made useless for defence and a centralised bureaucratic government replaced—at least in intention—the former feudal semi-autonomy of the mountain regions such as Krujë. Half-hearted attempts were made by the Turks to rebuild sections of the castle, after they had tightened their grip on the countryside, for they realised that sudden Balkan uprisings could overwhelm their government, and a defenceless castle is a doubtful asset to a ruling class.

The Sublime Porte was able to take Albania, and then to keep Albania by three methods. First, religious conviction on the model of the first great waves of Muslim imperialism, though only 3% of the population were converted to Islam in the first thirty-five years of Ottoman control, as opposed to 65% by the end of the seventeenth century. Second, formidable military power spearheaded by the first standing army in Europe. Third, a centralised administration with a clearly-delineated policy. At least thirty Grand Viziers were of Albanian descent, testifying to the fact that by no means all Albanians were enemies of Ottoman rule.

Compared with neighbouring lands, countries like Albania which remained under Ottoman control for many generations suffered social, economic and cultural retardation. The Sultan's claim to exercise total and absolute hegemony over all aspects of the lives of his subjects has been almost impossible to shake off, whether under Zog, the Italian colonists, the German colonists, or the Communists. Fear of the outside world begins at home, where one's house is built like a fortress, with room to accommodate livestock and foodstuffs under siege conditions. Village was suspicious of village, and mountain folk of lowlanders. When Muslim Albanians were treated as Turks, and Orthodox Albanians as Greeks, the Roman Catholic Church (exemplified by Bishop Fan Noli) became to a certain extent the saviour of the Albanian language and Albanian cultural traditions. This view is only partially true, since many priests set more store by their faith and allegiance to the Vatican than to their country, and the major part in preserving the Albanian way of life through the centuries can be attributed to the Bektashis, exemplified by the Frashëri family.

How can we people the palace and make it resound again to the human voice? One way is to turn to Edward Lear, who visited Krujë in 1848 with his Bulgarian interpreter (whom he calls Giorgio). He thought Krujë 'a charming little town all up in the sky . . . and it takes a good four hours to get up to it. On the highest point is now a beautiful palace belonging to Ali Bey—and there we went. He is a mere lad of 16 or 18, but most good-natured and well-bred—poor little fellow. The way he showed me the contents of a common writing-desk as wonderful curiosities, was droll enough. We could not say a word to each other but through Giorgio—so I drew for him, and amused him immensely by drawing a steam-carriage and saying—rattlerattlerattlerattle—and a ship-steamer—saying wishwashsquishsquash—at which the poor boy laughed immensely. All this is only odd because the state and ceremony about him makes such a contrast; when you see old men kneeling, and great brawny fellows looking frightened out of their lives when he speaks, you naturally suppose a superior being is before you—and are amazed to find he is little more instructed than they are . . . I gave Ali Bey a pencil and some needles for his mother, which delighted the poor child. He showed me all the rooms in the Harem, no one being there—so that is an opportunity I may never have again. Here this boy is to live, doing nothing but smoke from morning to night all his life!!'

As you wander around the ruins of Krujë castle, in which—as at Berat—a few hundred inhabitants eke out a meagre livelihood, you will come across a ruined church converted into a mosque, with an Osmanli date of reconstruction (mid-nineteenth century) engraved on a stone in the minaret. An old man with Muslim worry-beads smiled at me as I turned a corner alone: though not a Muslim, I sensed the isolation of his bent back and tired brown eyes and called out 'La ilahu ill' Allah!' (There is no God but Allah!). He embraced me with tears in his eyes, and fervently responded 'Wa Muhammadun rasul Allah!' (And Muhammad is His Prophet!), eagerly asking about my ancestry and purpose in coming to Albania. How could I say that I was an atheist? Shaban would only have thought me a spy, in league with the intolerant fanatics who prohibited him from worshipping his God. For humanists like myself, the opinion that there is no God carries with it the obligation to respect the opinions of all those who believe that there is a God.

So, hypocrite that I am, I recalled in halting Albanian my years at the feet of the imam of the Jam'a Ahmad Pasha Karamanli (itself an Ottoman foundation) in Libyan Tripoli, when I learnt what I know of the Qur'an al-Karim, and of the tenets of Islam, in those palmy days of King Idris' rule when infidels were permitted to enter the mosques of Libya and seek learning without prejudice. I spoke to the old Muslim of the great university of Fez, of Algerian Tilimsan, of the extraordinary Friday Mosque of Tunisian Qayrawan, of Sanusi mysticism at Jaghbub, of life in the crowded streets of Cairo and Beirut, of the mountain road that leads from Jeddah to Ta'if, and branches off to Makkah al-Mukarrimah. I told him of my Muslim friends in Indonesia, Malaysia and Singapore, and of the disastrous rule of Ayatollah Khomeini which threatened to encourage a Soviet invasion of Iran, and menaced Iraq and all the Sunni lands to the West. And then came inquisitive faces around the corner: I pretended to be playing with his grand-daughters Mimozë and Dafinë and gave them sweets. His moment of free speech amid the turbulence of the world outside Albania was over, but the handshake he gave recompensed my hypocrisy.

I found the baths built with bricks in the Byzantine manner, which are said to date from the time of Skënderbeg and were restored in 1967, to all appearances very competently.

On the west of the castle you will find the jewel of eighteenth-century architecture called the Dollma Tekke, a shrine of the Bektashi movement which included so many Albanian nationalists that it can fairly be described as the most representative nationalist movement in Albania.

Krujë. Former Bektashi tekke called Dollma.

While Orthodoxy was tied to Greek colonial aspirations, Catholicism to the Vatican, traditional Islam to Turkey, and the Party of Labour now in power to international communism, Bektashism in its peculiar Albanian form undermined all factions and opposites, mixed pagan, Christian and Muslim elements, and stood for mystic unity, intellectual honesty, and universal tolerance.

Hajji Bektash Veli was a thirteenth-century dervish from Khurasan (in modern Iran), who migrated to Anatolia and is buried at Hajji Bektash, between Kirşehir and Kayseri, where the governor of the Bektashi order, the Çelebi, used to reside. The basic teachings are Shi'a (acknowledging the twelve imams, and uniting Ali with Allah and Muhammad in a trinity), but pre-Islamic, pagan, and even Christian elements survive in a strange compound with popular mysticism and masonic-like secret signs of recognition. Bektashis confess their sins before a spiritual confessor and receive absolution; they attach little significance to formal prayers and none to Mecca; they do not veil their women; and they are not forbidden to drink alcohol. New members are received with the general distribution of wine, bread and cheese, which is obviously a survival of Holy Communion.

103

The Bektashis, who survive today in Albania (dare it be said?) despite the outlawing of all religious observance, teach that God is the divine spirit of goodness. Manifested not only in Christ, Muhammad, and other prophets, saints and leaders, the Bektashis—like Coleridge and Shelley—find God in nature: the mountains of Albania, Turkey and Greece easily lend themselves to pantheism. As Joseph Swire writes in *King Zog's Albania* (1937), a work which celebrates an Albania more tolerant than the one we visit today, the Bektashis then lived 'their philosophy from day to day with allowances for human frailties, teaching simplicity and brotherly love and gentleness towards all living creatures. Their beliefs are certainly confused with pagan superstitions and beliefs—many of these deliberately invented to identify (for gaining a hold over ignorant masses) some local saint or shrine or tribal deity with their own.'

Bektashis allow Christians and Muslims to join their order without giving up their other beliefs, they invite women to visit the tekkes, and believe that work is a duty by which man earns his right to eat. Bektashism was introduced into Albania by a dervish called Sari Sallteku, from Corfu, who founded seven tekkes in Albania, one being Sari Salik at Krujë. Other early tekkes were established at Tepelenë and Gjirokastër, but in the north and midlands the Muslim feudal chief Kara Mahmut Bushatli destroyed the Bektashi tekkes of Tirana, Krujë and Shkodër. In 1826 Sultan Mehmet II massacred his Bektashi janissaries, fearing their potential for subversion. The ally of the Ottomans, Ali Pasha, was secretly converted from orthodox Islam to Bektashism by Baba Shëmin of Krujë, who painstakingly re-formed the tekke and sect of Krujë and the tekke of Melçani at Korçë. When the Turkish government suppressed the dervish orders in September 1925, the then Albanian Çelebi chose to move the headquarters of the order to Tirana.

The legality of the Bektashi order in Albania was guaranteed by the Korçë Statutes of 1929, with clergy, members, and laymen. In the mid-1930s there were estimated to be 7,370,000 Bektashis, of whom 200,000 were Albanians. In 1952, the *Cahiers de l'Orient Contemporain* suggested that there were still as many as 30,000 Bektashis in Turkey alone. The reader is referred to J.K. Birge's authoritative *The Bektashi Order of Dervishes* (1937; reprinted 1982).

During Ottoman rule, the number of inhabited houses within the castle of Krujë fluctuated to a maximum of about eighty. Now there are roughly twenty occupied houses, many with a tiny private cultivated garden producing fruit and vegetables. Below the citadel, old-fashioned houses of two or three storeys stand firm amid olive groves. The ground floor was originally intended for keeping livestock and farm tools, while

Krujë. Restored Turkish bazaar.

residential rooms on the upper floors could be sealed off from intruders in case of need. You might occasionally catch a glimpse of woodcarving in a house interior, a domestic craft which reached its apogee at Krujë in the late eighteenth and earliest nineteenth century. At all events you will be able to explore the restored bazaar, partly covered with new roofs, on the way from the modern Hotel Skënderbeg to the castle. The narrow row of facing shops includes a hatter's, a silversmith's, a basket-maker's, and a felt-maker's. I chatted in Italian with a carpenter working on the restoration of a shop roof. 'Yes, the writers and thinkers are always scared, it seems to me, but as for us artisans, we work, eat, sleep and nothing can happen to us.' Above the bazaar a hoarding shouted in Albanian 'THE SEVENTH FIVE-YEAR PLAN WILL MAKE SOCIALIST ALBANIA MORE POWERFUL'. It seems that you have to convince an Albanian to believe political slogans by advertising just as in the West you have to convince consumers by advertising to buy a particular detergent. The difference is not in the billboards, which are equally ugly, but in the fact that in the West you are allowed to reject the ideology and the consumer goods touted on the hoardings.

Elbasan

The talk on the bus from Tirana to Elbasan was all about the new price cuts, announced the day before the Ninth Trades Union Congress was due to be held in Tirana. Instead of wage rises, which it is argued would lead to inflation and thus further impoverish the poorest, the Government decreed cuts in the prices of many commodities under the headline in *Zëri i Popullit*: ULJE E RE ÇMIMESH NE VENDIN TONE

('New Reduction of Prices in Our Country'), with the sub-heading translated as 'Prices Lower for Foodstuffs, Clothing, Most Consumer Goods, and for the Repair and Service of Goods'.

From 16 June 1982 a reduction of 35% was announced on local and imported radios, 30% on locally-made washing machines, 25—30% on national arts and crafts, 25% on plastic shoes, 22% on prams and baby-carriages, 20% on local tape recorders and children's toys, 18—20% on synthetic textiles and cotton fabrics made in Pogradec and Shkodër; 15—20% on leather shoes and sandals and crockery; 17% on plastic sandals; 15% on turkey and plastic consumer goods; 10—15% on men's and women's wrist-watches (the Albanian for this being the enchanting 'orë dore grash e burrash'); 11% on black-and-white television sets ('televizorë bardhë e zi'); 10% on all kinds of leather handbags and briefcases; 8—10% on chicken, goose, duck, and poplin and woollen goods; and 7% on locally-made bicycles. Furthermore, 135 tariffs for repair and servicing were reduced by 8 to 15%. An article in *Zëri i Popullit* dated 5 June 1982 claimed that these price reductions would save the Albanian consumer 75 million leks a year, a figure which might be questioned. What is not questionable, however, is the great propaganda value that price drops have in the Tirana press, which delights in underlining the economic crises constantly facing East and West alike. The modest four-page official paper devoted page one to the price cuts, nominations for Hero of Socialist Labour, and three features on the 9th Trades Union Congress. Page two printed articles on popular councils, moral norms for everybody, and photographs of fruit trees at Margegajt (Tropojë) and a laboratory assistant at Sarandë. Page three bore propaganda on finance by the Budget Director in the Ministry of Finance, an article on agriculture, with a photograph of a street in Shkodër beside a brief note on the restoration of monuments. Page four was devoted to Albania's interpretation of world news, from an article attacking the Guatemalan government to a feature on terrorism in Northern Ireland. The main articles concerned a crisis in the European Economic Community and a view by the commentator Qako Dango on a possible Peking-Washington-Tokyo political alliance. One is reminded that the press freedom of the West is an inconceivable fantasy to the whole of the Communist World, from Canton to Leipzig, and to the whole of the so-called Third World, from the Philippines to El Salvador. But even we should not become complacent, for nobody but the London *Morning Star* puts the Communist view daily before the British public, and bigotry against Communism in the United States did not die with Senator Joe McCarthy and the 'wanted' lists of former President Nixon.

Then we put down the morning paper and concentrated on the

54-kilometre run to Elbasan, quickly climbing above the barred compound of Comrade Enver and the Martyrs' Monument overlooking the city to the Gjergj Dimitrov State Farm, where huge orchards and vineyards green the once-bare rocks and barren soil. This is where our courier Lejla teaches English when she is not seconded for work with Albturist. Crossing the river Erzen, on the right we see the extraordinarily impregnable citadel of Petrelë. Try to persuade your driver and courier to take the 3km., road to Petrelë, for a visit is by no means an automatic privilege. The Emperor Justinian refortified an earlier stronghold here in the sixth century; nine centuries later Skënderbeg installed his sister Mamicë here to protect her while he was concentrating on attacking Ottoman forces. Remarkably well-preserved, Petrelë Castle is roughly triangular, with a watchtower and two water cisterns still discernible today.

Still following the course of Erzen river, which is 94km. long, you eventually leave it on ascending the Krrabë mountains. A lignite mine appears unexpectedly in Krrabë village, and then we cry 'please stop!' for

Krrabë Pass, between Tirana and Elbasan.

this breathtaking mountain landscape could be at the top of the world.

After Iba village, with its springs of icy water, we stop again for a breath of the purest air at the peak of Kaçulitë Pass, and then comes the descent to Elbasan and the oval Shkumbin Plain of Elbasan, about 16km. long and 6km. wide. As we sped comfortably in our air-conditioned coach at the end of a leisurely two-hour journey into the heat of Elbasan's mid-day, I re-read J. & C. Gordon's account of entering Elbasan in 1925, in their *Two Vagabonds in Albania* (1927): 'The voyager who dashes from Tirana to Elbasan, along the road, through the plains, a four-hour ride in a rickety Ford car, and who bravely risks one night at the Hotel Adriatik, does not get the quality of Elbasan. Elbasan is a town to loiter in... Perhaps the best place to get your Turkish coffee and cigarettes and contemplate is the hairdresser's shop. "Coffee *and* cigarettes" we write advisedly, for does not the Albanian proverb say "Kafa pa duhan si Turku pa iman" ("Coffee without tobacco is like a Turk without an imam")? And the barber's shop, much more gay than the café, was a place of resort for coffee-drinkers as well as for the unshorn. Or you could go to the silversmith's and begin a lengthy bargain for a pair of old silver buckles with the baptism of Christ crudely carved upon them or for a few old silver amulets.' In their day, the Gordons estimated a thousand shops for ten thousand inhabitants in a mercantile city situated almost precisely in the centre of Albania: not only on the classical Via Egnatia from Durrës to Ohrid, but also on the modern railway line from Durrës to Pogradec.

Possibly nowhere more than at Elbasan does one feel the force of historical aberration: that crucial moment when Muhammad became a Prophet in Arabia—that less crucial but no less fascinating moment in 1967 when Comrade Enver reversed the Muslim tradition of Central Albania and abolished the practice of Islam through the younger generation, emulating the Chinese Red Guards with the cardinal difference that in Albania the smaller number of youths were always under control from their masters in Tirana. For Elbasan was always the focus of easy fanaticism.

In Edward Lear's *Journal of a Landscape Painter in Greece and Albania* (1851), the nonsense-writer took the full force of Islamic fury against those who attempt in violation of Quranic law to draw, paint or sculpt living forms in impious emulation of Allah. At Ohrid he was pelted with sticks and stones and compelled, in a forlorn attempt at disguise, to wear a fez. In Tirana he was cursed by a Dervish. While at Elbasan—let us read his own account:

'No sooner had I settled to draw—forgetful of Bekir the guard—than forth came the population of Elbassan, one by one, and two by two, to a mighty host they grew, and there were soon from eighty to a hundred spectators collected, with earnest curiosity in every look; and when I had sketched such of the principal buildings as they could recognize, a universal shout of 'Shaitan!' burst from the crowd; and strange to relate, the greater part of the mob put their fingers into their mouths and whistled furiously, after the manner of butcher-boys in England. Whether this was a sort of spell against my magic I do not know; but the absurdity of sitting still on a rampart to make a drawing, while a great crowd of people whistled at me with all their might, struck me so forcibly, that come what might of it, I could not resist going off into convulsions of laughter, an impulse the Gheghes seemed to sympathise with, as one and all shrieked with delight, and the ramparts resounded with hilarious merriment.

'Alas! this was of no long duration, for one of those tiresome Dervishes—in whom, with their green turbans—Elbassan is rich—soon came up, and yelled 'Shaitan scroo! Shaitan!' ('The Devil draws! The Devil!') in my ears with all his force, seizing my book also, with an awful frown, shutting it, and pointing to the sky, as intimating that heaven would not allow such impiety. It was in vain after this to attempt more; the 'Shaitan' cry was raised in one wild chorus—and I took the consequences of having laid by my fez, for comfort's sake, in the shape of a horrible shower of stones, which pursued me to the covered streets, where, finding Bekir with his whip, I went to work again more successfully about the walls of the old city.

'Knots of the Elbassaniotes nevertheless gathered about Bekir, and pointed with angry gestures to me and my "scroo". "We will not be written down," said they. "The Frank is a Russian, and he is sent by the Sultan to write us all down before he sells us to the Russian Emperor".'

The Albturist Hotel Skampa (Albanian for Elbasan's classical name, Scampa), is situated opposite the main entrance to the formerly walled city. The Emperor Justinian started work on the fortress in the sixth century, but the Bulgarians overran the city and destroyed the fortress in the ninth century, razing the town in the process. Sultan Mehmet II chose Elbasan as his communications centre for attacks on Krujë, and rebuilt the fortress in 1466–7 with twenty-six towers, three gates, and a deep moat defending walls 362m. long x 327m. wide. Under Ali Pasha the defences were maintained and trade encouraged, but the Ottoman Reshid Pasha dismantled the fortress in 1832, leaving only its southern wall in a good state of preservation and only eight towers.

We were discouraged by the Albturist couriers from sauntering off on our own, but the official guide kept us waiting so long that in frustration I disobeyed the edict, stepping neatly over drunks taking a siesta on grass

Elbasan. Street scene, 1983.

below the castle walls. At the taxi rank I enquired the cost of a cab ride to Tirana: it was 500 leks for sole use, and 160 leks (more than £13) if I chose to wait for three other passengers. This seems very expensive by Albanian standards: virtually nobody but a foreigner could afford such a fare. Taxis for Korçë were also available.

High walls, shuttered windows, locked doors in the streets of the old fortress: how decorous and private are these houses and courtyards! One might almost be back in Ha'il or Buraidah, in Saudi Arabia. As Bernard Newman wrote, in *Albanian Back-Door* (1936): 'Twenty years ago Elbasan was almost a forbidden city. It was fanatically Moslem, and Christians were not welcome. The innumerable bandits in its region rendered it almost inaccessible; there was no semblance of a road to it, and it was necessary to hire an escort of Turkish cavalry before considering the journey. Even this by no means guaranteed your safe arrival—much more likely that your friends would receive one of your

Elbasan. Street plan, 1943. (Latest published) ▷

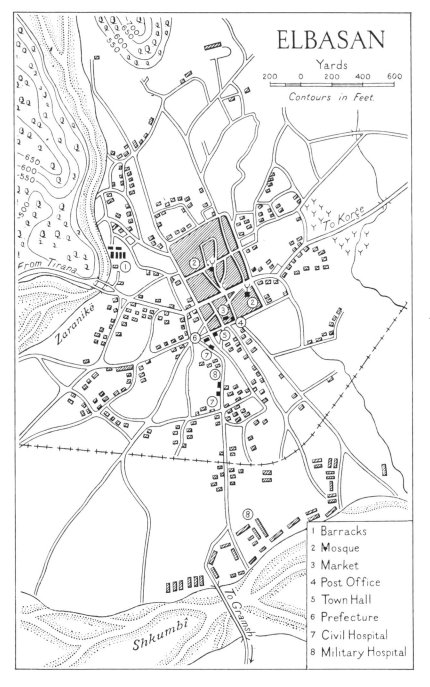

ELBASAN

Yards

200   0   200   400   600

Contours in Feet.

To Korçe

From Tirana

Zaranikë

Shkumbi

To Gramsh

1 Barracks
2 Mosque
3 Market
4 Post Office
5 Town Hall
6 Prefecture
7 Civil Hospital
8 Military Hospital

ears in a parcel, with a demand for a substantial ransom. If Albanian bandits did not rob you, then your Turkish cavalry escort would probably repair the omission. And now a man can ride to Elbasan alone! So could a woman, for that matter'.

I passed a deserted museum—the Muzeu i Luftës Antifashistë Nacional-Çlirimtarë—devoted to the War of National Liberation, with guns at peace in the sunny garden. A terrified cat scampered away from me like all the rats from a sinking ship. An urchin sped past clutching an unwrapped loaf. A donkey with an overloaded cart waited in the midday heat, without food or water. Elbasan closed in on me like a jail, as Albanian words whirled in my head: when we get tired, we stop and rest: 'Kur të lodhemi, pushojme pak dhe çlodhemi'.

Near the river I found an ancient mosque, and mourned the destruction of the beautiful bridge, which has been replaced by a more utilitarian model of no distinction. An old lady showed me the Orthodox church with arcaded sides: I did not press her to tell me of its contemporary use, but returned to the Hotel Skampa unhappy with the way in which the cur Elbasan has been whipped by successive masters. Employment has been found for Elbasani people at the Kombinati Metalurgjik Çeliku Partisë (Steel of the Party Metallurgical Combine) nearby, and at the oil refinery near the village of Çerrik not far from Elbasan: the first with Chinese aid and the second with Soviet aid. But the ABECOR group of European banks reported in its November 1981 newsletter that 'output of high-grade steel from the Elbasan iron and steel works has ceased because of a lack of skilled labour', following the withdrawal of Chinese aid in 1977–8 after repeated attacks by the Albanian leadership on Chinese political changes.

It is only fair to add that our view of Elbasan might have been more generous had we arrived in time for Rossini's *Berberi i Sevilles* given at the theatre of Elbasan on 3 and 4 June by Vlorë Dramatic Theatre, with Aferdita Tusle as Rosina and Adem Gjyzeli as Figaro. Ideologically, the Beaumarchais *Barbier de Séville* and the Rossini *Barbiere di Siviglia* are acceptable in Albania because they show the corrupt gentry (Bartolo) and clergy (Basilio) being outwitted by a man thought to be of the people (Figaro, even if we later discover that he is of quite different ancestry). Unfortunately for the ideology, the man of the people is simply serving the ends of the nobleman (Conte d'Almaviva), but let that pass...

7
Tirana

As a city and capital Tirana is an invention of the twentieth century, representing the Albanian will to be governed from the centre of the country rather than from the strategic strongholds of their past overlords: Shkodër in the north, Gjirokastër in the south, or Durrës on the Adriatic coast.

The mediaeval town gradually spread, with many private houses and shady gardens, around the Byzantine fortress constructed by Justinian in 520. The town declined to a few thousand, until in the second decade of the seventeenth century the local feudal leader Suleiman Pasha Mulleti built a mosque, public baths, and a market for agricultural produce from the surrounding villages. By the eighteenth century its position at the crossroads of all points on the Albanian compass caused gradual expansion, but the population in 1916 was still only 12,000. After the Congress of Lushnjë had decreed in 1920 that Tirana should become the new capital, the sleepy old town was transformed and Italian architects, respecting only the mosque of Ethem Bey of 1796–7, created a monumental centre called Piazza Scanderbeg, with an avenue running roughly southwards to the University of Tirana, opened in 1957. The State University of Tirana has 16,000 students. Students at all higher education centres spend seven months of each year at their Institute, two on production or construction, two on vacation, and one on physical education and military training. The southern avenue is flanked by ministries and other official premises, and—in the virtual absence of traffic—offers pleasant shade for the evening promenade. Here too is the Gallery of Figurative Arts, a kind of National Gallery dedicated to the dogma of socialist realism.

The Hotel Tirana is the most comfortable lodging in Albania, though the restaurant service is notably slow. It is centrally placed for all the shops, and stands on the main Skanderbeg Square like the National Bank, Ethem Bey Mosque, National Museum, and the huge Soviet-built Palace of Culture, which includes a theatre, opera house, cinema, conference halls, and the National Library. The Post Office stands near

113

Tirana. Skënderbeg Square from Hotel Tirana. The equestrian sculpture of Skënderbeg is in centre background.

the opposite corner, behind the National Bank, and is open from 6.30 a.m. to 9.00 p.m. daily. Foreigners are commonly seen out walking singly or in small clusters, so one feels far less inhibited than in Krujë or Elbasan. Taking a deep breath of fresh air, I walked out at 4.45, heading left from the hotel entrance towards the shaded avenues. The Italian-style Piazza Scanderbeg dwarfs the occasional lorry or diplomatic Mercedes: only in the evening do crowds emerge, filling the square not with the exuberant shouts and laughter of a Greek or Italian city but with a muted buzz, wary of being overheard as well as of being photographed or tape-recorded. At a bar I asked in Albanian for a bottle of apple juice at the cash desk and was given a receipt for my 2.50 leks (21 pence), which I then traded at the counter for a bottle and glass, much as if I were in Catanzaro or Amalfi. The Flora Bookshop was closed, but I found a Ma-Po open, and bought my wife embroidered cotton pillow-cases and a sheet from a stolid lady in black, who gratefully left a squad of heavyweight housewives assembled argumentatively around rolls of

Tirana. Hotel Tirana.

fabric on a counter. The sales-lady asked 'Mund të të ndihmoj?' (Can I help you?). 'Po: dua të blej çarçaf. Sa kushton?' (Yes: I'd like to buy a sheet. How much is it?')

The football season was over, and the Dinamo and Qemal Stafa stadia were closed until winter, so I decided to join a tour of the Ekspozita Kultura Popullorë Shqiptarë (Exhibition of Albanian Popular Culture), open 9—2 and 5—8 on Tuesdays, Thursdays and Sundays. All the captions are in Albanian, but even if you understand Albanian well, you may be prohibited from walking around on your own for security reasons. Intriguing open-plan displays recreate a shepherd's hut in the south, a Korçë reception room and southern reception-rooms, all with fine carpets. Evocative costumes include magnificent bridal gowns and grooms' suits, and as well as a butter-churn and a water-wheel one can examine saddle-bags for horses and donkeys, stonework, ironwork, ceramics, woodwork from Përmet, Dibra district and Berat, embroidery, woollen and cotton goods, Shkodër silk exported then as now to Austria and France, and such musical instruments as drums, pipes, castanets and the two-stringed lute.

The Shqipëria Sot (Albania Today) exhibition in the next pavilion is open from 9—12 a.m. on Tuesdays, Wednesdays, Saturdays and Sundays, and from 5—8 p.m. on Wednesdays and Sundays. Here you will find a predominantly industrial, technological and agricultural exhibition with the purpose of convincing the visitor that Albania is not only self-reliant (which is a half-truth) but is ideologically correct to remain self-reliant (which is questionable).

If you feel in need of green repose, there is a new lake (roughly forty hectares in area) east of the city with a park for recreation, and a botanical garden nearby, reputed to contain 1500 species of Albanian flora in an area of 15 hectares. For the untiring museumgoer I recommend as curiosities bordering on the bizarre in their delirious obsession with Leninism, Marxism, Albanianism and the Maoist-Stalinist cult of personality, such treasures as the Party Museum (Wednesdays and Fridays, 10—1 and 4—6, and Sundays, 10—1), the Lenin-Stalin Museum (Wednesdays and Fridays 10—1 and 4—6), and the Museum of Illegal Bases (Mondays and Fridays, 10—1, and Wednesdays, 10—1 and 4—6).

For shopping, the bazaar east from the Mosque of Ethem Bey offers a number of interesting state-run handicraft shops, where one can buy woodwork, glass, ceramics, shoes and slippers, ornamental boxes and shoulder-bags, decorative round water-bottles of carved wood, and rugs. The philatelic shop is northwest of the Hotel Tirana.

The new town in west Tirana, with its already-peeling and shabby apartment blocks, makes a depressing contrast to the animated central shopping quarter. The old town, north and east of Piazza Scanderbeg, still possesses a glint of the ancient Oriental charm which the indolent Ottomans brought with them. Old ladies in black hurry past with shopping bags stuffed with paper-wrapped fruit and vegetables.

I sat in the shade on a pile of rubble, opposite a white garden wall covered with indelible red slogans, and drafted a poem which began by pondering the motives for officially disfiguring one's city and concluded ruefully that you cannot ensure survival even by trying to co-opt posterity as a Party member.

Side Street, Tirana

By the whitewashed wall
shadows loom and pass:
the hands of the Party
cover it with slogans.

Rain and the rain of time between them
carve their own graffiti.

Into interstices of brick
penetrate stick fingers;
light at the other side
eventually lasers through.

Look! Old men who were the boys
who painted exhortations with red daubs
are carried to the cemetery,
one after patient one,
arthritic stick fingers
scarecrowing thin air.

Peeling red script their only epitaph,
they mingle at the very end,
dust upon windborne dust,
bereft even of shadows
under the rain of time.

A couple of girls skip by a half-open gate to a walled garden, while a mangy tomcat scampers past them, trying to seem invisible. A workman in old patched jeans carries a bucket with sand as if he's looking for somewhere to make concrete. Nobody laughs: I too can find nothing to make me wish I lived here, for even the weather in these Mediterranean latitudes can be oppressive in August and freezing in January.

In a *byrektore* I bit into a meat pie as I consulted Ronald Matthews on Tirana. His *Sons of the Eagle* (London, 1937) is the best memoir we have of the Albanian capital on the eve of World War II, when the leading hotel was the Italian-owned Continental and the Albanian-run International still rented you a bed in a room rather than a bedroom.

'The streets, lazy with heat, were emptying, for lunch-time is an official three-hour interval, except in the height of summer, when the Ministries start work at seven in the morning and there is no afternoon spell at all', writes Matthews of Tirana half a century ago. 'The native dishes on the tables—you have your choice of eating *alla franga* [in the European style. Ph.W.]—all betrayed that curious desire to hide the nature of the food served up that the eastern-bound traveller finds immediately he leaves Vienna. A very high proportion of the International's menu seemed to be modestly disguised in a cucumber or a vine-leaf cloak. Hardly any of the diners had wine before them: for most Albanians' drinking ends with the aperitif raki. Yet Albanian wine can be extremely good, a light but quite smooth burgundy. "The only trouble is you can never be certain what the next bottle is going to taste like," someone said. "We want more uniformity in production," he added, with the earnest sententiousness of a Chekhov character.

"Let's go and see one of the Ministries," Hiqmet suggested. On the steps a crimson-collared gendarme sprang to attention. A great deal of Tirana's population [20,806 was the 1936 figure. Ph.W.] seemed to have found its way into the cool corridors. Waiting outside almost every door was a resigned group of lean men and black-shawled women who turned incurious eyes at us as we passed.

"Good afternoon, gentlemen. You will have coffee?" the Director greeted us. It was a high, light room, looking out, away from the central square, over the New Quarter. Beyond it rose the smooth, tree-clad hills that form, opposite the mountain wall, the lower edge of the cup within which Tirana lies.' The Minister saw Matthews, telling him that, due to improved public security, there were only twenty murders a month. 'He told me of his efforts to educate the peasants out of their primitive cultivation: they would persist in ruining their olive crop by beating down the fruit from the trees... He told me of his plans to start co-operatives, to push forward land drainage: Albania's most fertile plains were in perpetual peril of inundation. He told me of the slow advance of the roads into mountain valleys where no wheeled vehicle could yet go. He was a good man among Albanian Ministers, everyone agreed. But over his brave words hung the cloud of an empty exchequer'.

Since current statistics in Albania are still measured for the sake of effect against a norm of the year 1938, it may be interesting to compare some points of Matthews' Tirana with the city of today, which has probably changed less in the interval than any other world capital. There is still the afternoon siesta in government offices and elsewhere. Entry to government ministries is far less free now than it was under King Zog, his Interior Minister from Shkodër Musa Juka, and Abdurrahman Mati. Wine is now widely drunk with meals, as raki still is as an aperitif. Public security has improved to the point where murder in the streets is almost unknown, but due to the ubiquitous Sigurimi and allied police forces unaccountable to public enquiry, there may be more lawlessness in 'law enforcement' than ever before. Co-operatives have not only been started: they have been completed so finally that very little private property of any kind remains. Land drainage has also been achieved with dramatic success. The roads may still be appalling by western European standards, but they must surely be better than they were in 1938. As for the 'empty exchequer', reliant then on the Italian lira as Mexico is now on the U.S. dollar (having borrowed £46,000 million in the last few years to bolster industrial and agricultural development), one can quote from the official *Shqiptarja e Re* as follows: 'Under capitalism the prices of goods fluctuate spontaneously according to demand and supply at a time when fierce competition for maximum profits is raging. In the People's Socialist Republic of Albania supply and demand are administered by the state which plans the volume of production and the amount of mass consumer goods sold in compliance with the needs and purchasing power of the population, which represents the demand for commodities. The purchasing power of the population is met constantly, without let-up and zigzags, through the necessary fund of goods to be sold, which outstrips the purchasing power of the population. [But there *are* shortages and a limited range of goods produced. Ph.W.] In our planning practice, to achieve harmony between the economy and monetary circulation, a system of material and financial balance is used to maintain due proportions between accumulation and consumption, between the monetary income of the population and the increase in labour productivity. The state economic plan ensures also the monetary means necessary for extended socialist reproduction in compliance with the needs of the people's economy.' [Yet the figures available refute this doctrinaire statement: in the 5th Five-Year Plan (1971–5), planned growth in national income was 55–60% but actual growth only 38%; planned growth in investment was 64% (actually 53%); industrial production 61–66% (52%); agricultural production 65–69% (33%); retail sales 36–39% (35%) and real per capita income 14–17% (14%). Dresdner Bank data, 1979.]

'The stability of the monetary system in the People's Socialist Republic of Albania is also due to the fact that in the state budget income is higher than expenditure. The expenditure envisaged under the budget is met by the income from the socialist economy which is always growing, without

Tirana. Ethem Bey Mosque.

issuing currency above the limits needed by extended socialist reproduction. Strict implementation of this monetary policy avoids circulation of surplus currency, averts price rises as are noted in capitalist economies, while not affecting the living standard of the working people, but on the contrary raising it systematically in line with the tasks laid down under the state plan.'

I asked our couriers for permission to attend the comedy *Kështu të dua* (I Love You Like That) at 7 p.m. at the Teatri Popullor, and both Lejla and Flora came with us to the theatre, which is reached from the Hotel Tirana by crossing Skanderbeg Square immediately in front of the Palace of Culture, and passing behind the eighteenth century Mosque of Hajji Ethem Bey to the corner of the Avenue of National Martyrs.

A mainly young audience in shirt-sleeves and festive mood was entertained with the problem 'How shall we marry off Dasho?' Since *Kështu të dua* bears as much relation to the popular conception of grim Stalinist Albania as Bondi Beach to the Kremlin, it is worth describing Pëllumb Kulla's comedy in some detail. Violeta Manushi as the materfamilias has already succeeded in marrying off one son and her two daughters (Margarita Xhepa as Floresha and Drita Haxhiraj as Dhurata), but Dasho remains single. He hopes to marry Mamica (Marjeta Ljarja, the actress who took the part of Jeta in the film *The Girl with Red Ribbons*). Her father is played by Sulejman Pitarka, a well-known senior dramatist whose play *The Fisherman's Family* has been translated into English, but so unidiomatically as to be unactable. He disapproves so strongly that Dasho is in despair. When Mamica comes to call, Dasho (played by Agim Qirjagi) decides to ask her to stay with him, and locks her in to prevent her going back, but she runs off.

In scene two Dasho, an architect and interior designer, calls Mamica's brother into his office to accuse him of bad work. The youth (a comic figure not unlike the Alain of *La fille mal gardée*) breaks down and weeps, his response to any awkward situation. 'Why does he cry?' enquires Dasho. Because he cries every time he sees bad work, and as all his work is bad, he is always crying. He is soon to take his examinations and interviews to qualify as an architect and interior designer, and is afraid he will fail, since Dasho is his examiner.

Mamica's father (MF), an influential citizen, knocks peremptorily on Dasho's door, and asks to buy furniture quickly instead of going on the waiting list like everyone else. 'But our furniture is sold only to the people', argues Dasho. MF stamps out angrily, shouting that he too is one of the people.

The scene changes to MF's private house and garden in Tirana, showing him to be a wealthy man. He tells Mamica that she must never see Dasho again, for he is disagreeable and unworthy of her. His son then interrupts them and tells his father that he is worried about his exam tomorrow. 'Never mind', gesticulates MF, 'I will fix it for you: who is the examiner?' 'Dasho!' 'Oh, you are sure to fail, then.' Now the son reveals that plans have been approved to pull down MF's private house to make way for a people's apartment block. 'Never mind', says MF, 'We can fix it: who do we have to see?' 'Dasho!' As Dasho appears from the wings to court Mamica, MF takes out his shotgun and fires. There is a crash in the wings and Mamica's brother dashes over, returning with the corpse of...a sheep! The son is weeping: 'It is forbidden to shoot sheep in the city!'

MF now realises that he is cornered on all sides and resolves to have Dasho as an ally in the family rather than as an enemy outside, so he comes to pay a preliminary visit on Dasho's mother. Mamica, who was already there, hides in the kitchen. Dasho finally arrives, in a state of nervous tension, but his mother solves everything by granting permission for Mamica to marry her son. Now Mamica emerges from the kitchen, blushingly confessing that she had been there all the time. 'I know,' winks MF: 'I recognised your bicycle outside!'

With a set by Shaban Hysa, and production by Esat Oktrova and Avni Resuli, *Kështu të dua* remains my second most treasured memory of Albania, the first being Gjirokastër's streets and houses. The acting was professionally-timed and polished, the costumes entirely appropriate, and the social satire not as one-sided as in other films and plays emanating from the state-controlled media. Scene-changing was deftly unobtrusive, characterisation was not all monochromatic, and the infectious laughter of the audience took our minds off the reality of a city where everyman has a spy at his shoulder, where the leaders of the nation cannot relax, and where anybody who tries to obtain a town-plan is suspected of ulterior motives.

The following night, our band of dedicated theatregoers by now reduced to three, we visited the Teatri Popullor for the propaganda play *Komunistet* by Ruzhdi Pulaha starring Robert Ndrenika and Margarita Xhepa. *Komunistet* is set in Tirana and Korçë during the Italian occupation of 1939–42, and is based on Comrade Enver's *Kur lindi Partia* ('When the Party was born'). While this interpretation of Albanian history has undeniable fascination, because it shaped the way in which Albanians have been taught to view the past, it must not go unchallenged. Anton Logoreci has observed, in *The Albanians* (1977), that 'the Albanian official record of the founding of the communist party and of Hoxha's election as leader in 1941 was completely rewritten, under his supervision, after Yugoslavia's break with Russia in 1948. The

Tirana. Inside a model kindergarten.

crucial rôle played by the Yugoslavs [and one must cite in justification the names of Dušan Mugoša and Miladin Popović, both sent by Tito to unite the warring Albanian factions] in this and subsequent events has disappeared altogether. Whenever Yugoslav political figures or Yugoslav policies are mentioned in Albanian publications they are made to serve as butts for censure and vituperation.'

Furthermore, one cannot take very seriously any play which offers only one side of a picture: Othello is not *merely* jealous and criminally cruel, but also tender and difficult to convince of Desdemona's alleged guilt. The production by Piro Mani is foolishly rhetorical, depending on a pink glow for heroism, fixed postures for determination, and mere shouting for conviction. The cause of truth is not served by such ranting, but neither is a vital acting tradition, which depends on a wide range of emotions and styles.

Next morning we were invited to inspect the Kopshti i Femijëvë (Kindergarten) nr.9 of Tirana, the head teacher being Mrs Margarita Xhahari. She and her teachers (two to a class of 27 or 28) run a kindergarten for 121 children between the ages of 3 and 6 six days a week, with no annual holidays, for one or both parents will be working throughout the year, and consequently require to have their children looked after during the day. Children are accepted in two shifts: either 6—noon or 1—7. They eat in the school, unless their parents call to take them home, and sleep after lunch in cots. Indoor plants make the sunny rooms pleasant, as do the open windows and scrubbed floorboards, but what makes the flesh creep is the total indoctrination system from the age of three. Political slogans on the walls are repeated mindlessly by the group (what three-year-old can understand a slogan?), and tots rush to recite party songs in praise of workers, in praise of Children's Day (1 June), and in praise of the Party of Labour and its leader Comrade Enver. Fresh-faced giggling infants in white smocks sing of the deeds of the partisans forty years ago.

We trooped upstairs, after applauding the little helpless mites, and found another twenty-eight were ready and waiting to recite a poem on the courage of Albanian soldiers, brandishing toy rifles, and on the love of Comrade Enver towards children, whom he has called 'the fragrant blossoms of our nation'.

The curriculum of the kindergarten consists of Albanian language, maths, drawing, building bricks, patriotism, singing and poetry. Attendance costs nothing, and is voluntary, for compulsory schooling starts at the age of six or seven, but the sixty-three kindergartens in Tirana are well patronised. Parents' committees co-operate in organising children's festivals and excursions, and in contributing additional toys. Equipment seemed adequate, and the little tin and wooden toys were plentiful enough. But childhood should be an age free from political, religious or moral indoctrination. All societies feel the necessity for some kind of more or less formal initiation ceremony at puberty, the transition from childhood to adult life, in order that one generation shall pass its accumulated experience to the next, even if the teaching is purely ritual or symbolic; but to stress unequivocal worship of the leader, whether Saddam Hussain in Iraq, the Pharaoh in ancient Egypt, or Mao in recent Chinese history, cannot be too strongly condemned.

Albanian Life (October–December 1976) is quite open about indoctrination from the age of three: 'The work for the all-round communist education of the children is carried out not only during lessons but also during all the free time which children spend at a kindergarten. This work is closely linked with the work which is done by the family and society and the various artistic and cultural institutions, and means of propaganda and information, etc.' I am not sure what is implied by the word 'etc.'.

It was this experience more than any other that finally condemned hard-line Albanian nationalism in the minds of the majority of our group whose minds were still open. I saw furrowed brows, expressions of anger, and sardonic ridicule on the faces of British and Commonwealth visitors. Few gave immediate vent to their fury, but it emerged as we split

Tirana. National Museum.

up into clusters inside the National Museum, on Skanderbeg Square, our next call. Past the digital clock on the National Bank, under the insistent banners LONG LIVE THE PEOPLE'S REPUBLIC OF ALBANIA and RAISE HIGH THE REVOLUTIONARY SPIRIT, we entered the massive, cool interior of the new National Museum, replacing the small Archaeological and Ethnographical Museum on the university campus.

The colossal National Museum recently opened on Skanderbeg Square may stand in proportion to the Palace of Culture, with the Hotel Tirana between them, but its monumentality is strangely at odds with the scale of the nation, as though a whale had been stranded in a village stream. Its function seems at first sight scientific, but gradually one realises that its content and ideology is heavily influenced by the regime—as though the Louvre were to replace its galleries of foreign art with 'heroes of the Resistance' and huge displays for de Gaulle and Giscard d'Estaing, which in turn were to fill the warehouses to make way for Mitterrand's exploits. A statue of Comrade Enver, greater than life size, confronts the visitor on entering, and anti-aircraft guns restore the feeling of siege experienced on country roads.

A Stone Age cave near Korçë is reconstructed near graffiti from Lepënicë dating from 6000 B.C. The spread of Illyrian tribes is illustrated by crude ceramics from Kamnik (Kolonjë). The New Stone Age in Albania is dated 6000–2600 B.C., and the Copper Age from 2600–2100

125

B.C. Fine ceramics and bronze tools, swords and daggers are shown from the Bronze Age (2100–1100 B.C.), and the Iron Age (1100–500) is particularly well displayed. The Greek colonies provide materials (from Amantia and Antigonea) such as Greek red-figure vases, while a superb Head of Artemis from Apollonia indicates the excellence of some Greek provincial art. Counterpointing the Greek treasures are the spearheads and helmets of the native Illyrians whom we have been taught by the Greeks to consider inferior. Amphorae covered in sea-shells rescued from wrecks and the seabed consort oddly with an Illyrian farmer's sickle and hoe-head.

Mute prehistory on the ground floor gives way to a selection of mediaeval Albanian artefacts on the first floor, starting with the obligatory slave-chains and shackles from Berat, not far from a fifteenth-century icon of St George from Berat. Halberds and similar weapons help to tell the story of Skënderbeg as though he were in some meaningful way the true ancestor of Comrade Enver. Arms of the sixteenth and seventeenth centuries lovingly polished and sharpened by the Museum's expert staff are set beside a view of Sinan's elegant sixteenth-century mosque in Prizren. A properly-balanced view would show more than the single model of domestic architecture of the age in this gallery, but if ever the Albanians create an open-air museum near Tirana on the lines of Arnhem or Ironbridge, an abandoned *kullë* from the north and a recreation of a Gjirokastër mansion would be worth a hundred illustrations. Three of the best icons by David Selenicasi (eighteenth century) are shown against one by his sixteenth-century predecessor Onufri. Best represented by the frescoes on the walls of the Church of St Nicholas in Voskopojë (Moskhopolis) dated to 1726, David brings a fresh breeze of realism to the rigid orthodoxy of hieratic Byzantinism. But whereas by provincial Albanian standards, David marks a step forward, one must realise that the 1720s in Europe have seen all the lessons of the High Renaissance learnt, absorbed, and pursued into the strange new paths of Boucher, Watteau (who died so young in 1721), Canaletto and other *vedutisti* springing from the example of Carlevaris, Giambattista Tiepolo, and Hogarth.

To emphasise the essentially agricultural economy of Albania—uninterrupted from Illyrian times to the present day—we are shown a table analysing the economy into three sectors: agriculture, 45%; livestock, 40%; and handicrafts of all kinds, 15%. Examples of such crafts are cups, drinking bowls, and daggers with sheaths encrusted in precious metals, followed by mountain costumes. Patriots approved at the present day and thus featured here include the Bektashi Abdyl Frashëri, Jani Vreto, and Pashko Vasa. A huge display of carefully-maintained nineteenth-century rifles is intended to illustrate the struggle for independence: relics of the Bektashis Sami and Naim Frashëri include a few of their books. We pass to the twentieth-century struggle for independence, with a bust of Avni Rustemi and details of the Vlorë events of June—August 1920. The struggle against the Italian and German occupation forces is narrated (like all the captions, solely in Albanian) with such illustrative matter as flags, guns, and a copy of *Das Kapital.* Here is an Olivetti typewriter that once belonged to Comrade Enver, of the same vintage as the one just seen in Sarandë's Banka e Shtetit. Souvenirs of the Communist agitator Qemal Stafa include a German-Albanian dictionary with his address shown as Via Ricasoli 61, Florence—a strange mercantile address for a man who sought to overthrow private enterprise. (And then one recalls that Venice, Bologna, and Naples too have all now fallen under the sway of Communist city councils.)

A great deal of space is allotted to photographs and explanations of parts of recent Albanian history, and much else is ignored. It would be interesting to see a 'revised version' of the National Museum in thirty years' time.

Radio programmes from Tirana start at 5 a.m. with news and popular folk music, on 221, 275 and 463 metres. Until close-down at 11 p.m. the schedules are dominated by domestic news, folk music, plays, sport, and magazines of literary, musical and cultural interest. Political, economic and industrial and agricultural items are scattered throughout the day, but there is a notable shortage of foreign news and views, reflecting governmental xenophobia.

Regional radio stations operate in Berat, Gjirokastër, Korçë, Kukës, Sarandë and Shkodër.

There is only one television channel, too, and anyone on the work-shift from 5 to 10.35 p.m. will miss even that. A typical schedule will consist of sport (5.15—7.00); a film for children (*Pinocchio*, say) from 7.00—7.30; a concert by Kosova artistes (7.30—8.00); a magazine programme (8.00—8.30); a political or social documentary (8.30—8.50); a concert by the Skënderbeu Ensemble of Korçë (8.50—9.50); circus acts (9.50—10.20); news (10.20—10.35). Close-down. The omission of programmes from overseas is peculiar only in the western context: most Communist countries avoid showing films depicting expensive consumer goods, first-rate clothes, large cars, fine food, and luxurious houses. Discontent may be aroused all too easily in the working class, whose function is to keep industry and agriculture moving.

Those of us who expressed a wish to see the evening news on Albanian television were conducted to one of the bedrooms with a TV set. Our couriers interpreted in general terms but there was no need to interpret the long minutes of deafening applause when Comrade Enver Hoxha entered the hall where the 9th Trades Union Congress was being held. Since Comrade Enver, unlike 99% of Albanians, wore a tie and a well-cut suit, it seemed as though the applause may have been addressed equally to his valet.

Carefully selected representatives from all over the country had been filmed before their enthusiastic send-off by fellow-workers in field and factory, school and hospital. (We were to see the enthusiastic ceremony of welcoming back the delegates on our return to Shkodër). But let me leave a description of what we saw to the journalist on ATA (Agence Telegraphique Albanaise), whose information bulletin in French is placed on Tirana hotel lounge- and bar-tables for all to study.

(Tirana, 6 June 1982)

'The 9th Trades Union Congress of Albania began its deliberations at Tirana today. The delegates and guests stood to greet with lengthy applause the entry into the hall of the First Secretary of the Central Committee of the Party of Labour of Albania Enver Hoxha, the President of the Presidium of the People's Assembly Haxhi Lleshi, the President of the Council of Ministers Adil Carcani, and other leaders of the Party and the Government. The Congress is also attended by several trades union delegations from various parts of the world. The Congress was declared open by Hysen Veizi, Hero of Socialist Labour and worker of the 'Steel of the Party' iron and steel works at Elbasan. After the election of the congress officers and approval of the orders of the day, Rita Marko, Member of the Politburo of the Central Committee of the Party of Labour of Albania and President of the Central Council of Albanian Trades Unions delivered a report "On the activity of the Central Council of the Albanian Trade Unions and the Tasks of the Trade Unions in Applying the Decisions of the 8th Party Congress".'

So *that* is why a Trades Union Congress is held: to apply the decisions of the previous Party Congress! The previous TV programme had been a circus, this time taking place in Durrës, in a big top.

Since it is formally recognised by the Albanian Government that the country is unique in its political system, taking collectivism to its fullest extent, Albturist arranged for us, in a lecture room within the Hotel Tirana, a talk on the political and social system by Comrade Paskal, Director of Legal Science in the Supreme Court. Now 55, he belongs to an ethnic minority. At the outbreak of the Revolution he was washing dishes in a restaurant belonging to a capitalist: he then took the first year of law study at evening school, and graduated as a lawyer. He is not appointed to the Supreme Court, but elected, and believes that this system must be better than the British system, for in Albania it is claimed that the people are truly represented by the people. This begs the question of how far the electors are competent to judge the relative worth of candidates, but there is certainly some good to be said on both sides.

Comrade Paskal described the People's Assembly, Albania's highest form of parliament. Candidates to elections, held every four years, must be 18 years of age or older. Voting, said not to be compulsory as it is in Australia for example, is for any one candidate from two or three proposed by the people in each electoral zone. Roughly 30% of the Assembly are party members. 'Comrade Enver is not the head of state, but merely the Secretary of the Party of Labour'. No reference was made to the inner cabinet meetings over which Comrade Enver presides. Nor to the fact that Albania's first general election under Communist rule, held on 2 December 1945, was confined to candidates of the Democratic Front, a body controlled by the Communist Party, and that the 82 candidates were all party members or fellow-travellers. Such an election ran directly counter to the Communist Party's own declaration at Berat in 1944 guaranteeing free elections and other civil and human rights. The same conditions have applied in every subsequent election, as can be judged from the Government publication *35 Vjet Shqipëri Socialiste* (Tirana, 1979):

Date of Election	% of Populace Voting	% of Votes for Democratic Front Candidates
2 December 1945	89.81	93.16
28 May 1950	99.43	98.28
30 May 1954	99.92	99.86
1 June 1958	99.98	99.96
3 June 1962	99.99	99.99
10 July 1966	99.99	99.99
20 September 1970	100.00	100.00
6 October 1974	100.00	100.00
12 November 1978	99.99	100.00

A footnote states: 'The brilliant results at the elections constitute the expression of steel-like unity of the people around its party of Labour'. Or one might suggest that in the absence of alternative candidates, the result is a foregone conclusion, and that the universal participation claimed means that no Albanian could have been abroad, ill, or absent from the election for any other reason on the above days in question.

The same source casts implicit doubt on the assertion that the untutored proletariat runs the country, for their educational background of deputies to the Assembly has become more not less élitist over the past 16 years recorded:

Date of Election	% of college graduates	% of secondary-school graduates	% of elementary school graduates	% without elementary education
3 June 1962	44.4	22.9	18.2	14.5
20 September 1970	50.0	25.0	24.0	1.0
6 October 1974	60.0	20.8	17.6	1.6
12 November 1978	72.8	15.2	10.4	1.6

It must be remembered that the University of Tirana was not founded until 1957, so the nation has enjoyed barely a quarter of a century of tertiary education.

Comrade Paskal stressed the part that the people play in the life of the nation at all levels, the strength of the women's movement, financial stability, equality of income, the highly satisfactory state of public order, and the excellent security enjoyed by Albanians and tourists alike, due to the vigilance of the network of plain-clothes agents and informers known as Sigurimi, associated with the frontier guards, people's police equivalent in some ways to a western police force, and the unpaid auxiliary police, consisting of all able-bodied civilians who serve an obligatory two months every year, and can be distinguished by their red armband.

Albania's legal system can only be properly appreciated if one casts aside western preconceptions, and relates it to the Soviet legal system from which it is derived. For example, although the Constitutions of 1946 and 1976 guarantee the right of a defendant to legal aid, in practice this right has been suspended for several years. For another example, following the explosion at the Soviet Embassy in 1951, a decree passed the death penalty, without recourse to process of law, for anyone 'engaged in terroristic activities', and a special tribunal set up to deal summarily with all such cases. For a third example, a 1968 law on court reorganisation decrees that 'people's courts will be guided in their activities by the policy of the Party'. For a fourth example—if more were needed—the 1976 Constitution states that 'the courts protect the socialist juridical order, strive to prevent crime, and educate the masses of working people to respect and implement socialist law, relying on their active participation'. In other words, everyone must be an informer.

Comrade Paskal smiled tolerantly at imputations of intolerance. 'Oh no', he replied to a question about the prevention of divine worship, 'we are so tolerant that I see my own mother daily make the sign of the Cross, and nobody stops her, even though it could be embarrassing.

After all, she is 80 and one must always respect the old'.

As a divorce-court judge, Comrade Paskal has spent the last 27 years in advising married couples not to separate—it disrupts the solidity of the social fabric. 'Grounds for divorce here are adultery, lack of love, incompatibility.' 'But not because the wife is barren?' asked someone innocently. 'Of course not', snorted Comrade Paskal. 'I have had only one such case brought to me, of a man trying to divorce his wife because he wanted a son and she could not produce children. What happened? I took the husband and wife to one side and persuaded them to adopt a child. Now they too are happy.'

'Courts do not deal with offenders below the age of fourteen: such delinquents are sent to an "education colony". Here, a vocational labour camp is equipped with a secondary educational school, so that when they come back out into society they have both scholastic and practical attainments. In our courts we try to give petty offenders advice or just fine them. If they persist, they go to labour camps. Imprisonment is up to a maximum of 25 years. Yes, the death penalty exists for murderers and traitors. Priests have been executed for distributing arms to groups of traitors. The average wage of 380 leks a year reduces the causes of envy and hatred, for nobody earns more than twice as much as anyone else. We have the lowest crime rate in the world, for all our people are keen to stamp out anti-social behaviour in all fields. We are proud of not having large private houses, but everyone has at least a room to live in. We may have no private cars, but food is adequate to keep everyone nourished. We have outlawed pornography, indecent dress, pop music, prostitution, and singing in the streets'.

Someone asked hopefully if Albania had any cartoons or jokes that were not political, having spent ten days so far searching for one in vain. Comrade Paskal turned pensive. 'Ah,' he exclaimed, brightening. 'One by one the Soviet bloc expands, taking in all of Asia, all of Africa, all of Europe, Australia, South America, Central America, until they come to the United States, and then stops. A journalist meets a member of the Soviet Politburo in the street by chance and asks why the Soviet bloc had not also swallowed up the U.S.A. The commissar opens his eyes in astonishment at the naïveté of the journalist. "Don't be silly!" he replies. "How else could we buy enough grain?".'

After the lecture, with polite questions parried neatly by the experienced lawyer, we took lunch with him in the Hotel Tirana, and he again waxed eloquent about the good life in Albania, based on a guaranteed minimum of food, shelter and public security. After an excellent meal, he was driven away in his government Volvo. The next car up is a Mercedes.

Tirana. Palace of Culture on Skënderbeg Square, with the Editor of *Drita* and the poet Bardhyl Londo.

Three of our group were privileged to meet Xhevat Lloshi, Editor of the cultural weekly *Drita* ('Light'), Rruga Konferenca e Pezës 4, Tirana, and his colleague Bardhyl Londo, a journalist and poet. The circulation of *Drita* is 20,000, which is very high indeed—equivalent to the entire population of Tirana in 1936. The magazine, in newspaper format and on poor-quality newsprint, is devoted to both literature and the arts. Its sixteen pages dated 6 June 1982 were devoted to the Trades Union Congress (pp.1–2); monumental sculpture (pp.3–4); new professional and amateur music productions (p.5); a discussion on the artistic treatment of contemporary themes (p.6); problems of the drama (p.7); illustrations from a new book entitled *The Working Class in the Figurative Arts*, poems by Petrit Ruka and Myrteza Kasi, and a story by Bahri Myftari (pp.8–10); new documents on the struggle for Independence (p.11); the restoration of ancient monuments (p.12); and articles and notes in brief. A token nod at foreign literature consists of translations by Klara Kodra from Dante, Cavalcanti, Marcantini and Pascoli, all names being respelt in Albanian phonetics.

Comrade Xhevat explained that he had been a scientific worker in Archives Research at the Institute of Linguistics at Tirana University when nominated to the editorship of *Drita*. A small, stocky figure of immense energy and self-assurance, Comrade Xhevat answered our questions with good humour and understanding patience, given our colossal ignorance of Albanian realities and the world in general.

'The arts in Albania are divided into three sectors', he began. 'The first is living folklore, unique to Albania, which is the property of everyone, and evolves without instruction. The second sector is the Amateur Movement, which arises organically and spontaneously from the desire of the people to unite in groups and companies. Organisational help may be given to forming such companies, providing methods for ensuring that sufficient authentic costumes are prepared, adjusting the words of folksongs to suit contemporary conditions, and choreographing dances which might be forgotten. Festivals are produced nationally to bring together dance groups and to ensure continuity of tradition from one generation to the next. The third sector is that of the professional, whether as a member of the officially-approved Writers' Union, sculptor, painter, singer or actor. The film industry belongs almost exclusively to the professional sector. *Drita* is predominantly concerned with this last sector. Art must be cultivated professionally as well as enjoyed at the pre-amateur and amateur levels.'

'No child is ever born believing in Socialism: it has to be taught,' suggested one of the British guests. 'No', returned Comrade Xhevat, 'it has to be *lived*'. He put questions to embarrass us: we could not answer them because to reply would call in question our tolerant, complex, pluralist society with its inherent tensions and inconsistencies. If one does not have a vigilant informer in every house, crime is likely to pass undetected more easily. If one encourages Asians to seek asylum from Uganda for humanitarian reasons, then one will invite racial tension in certain communities. If one permits anyone to start up a business for his own gain or his own satisfaction, he may succeed or fail, but you will never achieve equality of income.

'Why', enquired Comrade Xhevat, 'is the U.K. spending £1,000 million and more on a neo-colonialist war about the distant Falklands when Albania does not even lay claim to Corfu, just a few miles offshore, or to Kosova in Yugoslavia, with huge numbers of Albanian-speakers?'.

'Why is the level of crime so high in Britain, when in Albania it is virtually non-existent?'

'Why—when there are no beggars in the whole of Albania—should there be so many at and around the entrance to Westminster Abbey?'

'Why is the level of unemployment so high in Britain, when every

Albanian is guaranteed a job, and indeed *must* work unless physically or mentally disabled?'

It is impossible to show an Albanian that the conflicts between British trade unions and management result from free negotiation and a history of victory after victory by the unions to achieve such a catalogue of successes that the balance of power (and thus of the British economy) is now in their hands, while in Albania the trades union movement is entirely in the hands of the Party of Labour, and a strike is not only unthinkable, but actually illegal.

So I ended our discussions with a question born of the marriage between humility and curiosity. 'Ever since my daughters have been old enough to read, Shoku Xhevat, I have encouraged them to investigate a myriad ways of thinking and believing, including all philosophies and religions, atheism and pantheism, Japanese and Indian, Christian and Muslim. They have explored the Communism of Brezhnev and Castro, the way of Lao Tzu, the sanctity of San Francesco d'Assisi, and the everyday heroism of Anna Frank and Edith Cavell. Now, we have seen that in Albania, as in most countries, there is only one acceptable doctrine, and all the rest are declared anathema. Would you explain where you think I have gone wrong?'

'Of course, sorry! If you see a child treading on broken glass with bare feet, do you say: please continue in your own way without advice from me?' 'No, but that is hardly . . .'

'Well, sorry! In just the same way we must remove the dangers from the child's *mental* path. You agree with me that religion is unnecessary and historically simply an aberration, deriving from man's original awe before the unknown. So you must also agree that one must stop children from following such erroneous doctrines. Historically, Marxism-Leninism has replaced all other philosophies: it is comprehensive, accurate, and internally consistent . . .' 'Like a good index', I murmured.

'Sorry? There is no need to teach mistaken beliefs, but only the correct one. Then each culture will express Marxism-Leninism in its own way. Sorry: don't misunderstand me. We do not wish to export Albanian Marxism-Leninism as the Soviets wish to export their own brand, and the Cubans wish, and so on and so forth. Let France and Italy take their own Marxist-Leninist paths to the future: they will surely be different from ours.'

We three Britons filed out, ruminating on the Albanianism propounded by the Editor of *Drita* in each issue of his cultural magazine, and by the Editors of *Puna* (Labour), *Rruga e Partisë* (The Party Way), *Zëri i Popullit* (The Voice of the People), *Bashkimi* (The Union), *Zëri i Rinisë* (The Voice of Youth), *Ylli* (The Star), *Nëntori* (November),

Shqiptarja e Re (New Albania), *Pionieri* (Pioneer), *Probleme Ekonomike* (Economic Problems), and all the other official journals.

The theoretical objection to Albanianism as a dogma and way of life can be stated in the same way that one can state the objection to any dogma and any stubborn patriotism. No dogma is correct at all times and in all places, and is often wrong most of the time, as circumstances change; and patriotism is, in Dr Johnson's memorable words, the last refuge of a scoundrel. In other words, the xenophobia marking non-pluralist societies like Khomeini's Iran or Hoxha's Albania is a form of collective egotism. Patriotism has its vital place in preserving the will-to-independence of a subservient people, like France under Hitler or Albania under the brief Nazi rule, but once independence is attained the time has surely come to offer one's citizens their economic and intellectual freedom.

Albanians are restricted in opportunities to travel abroad, in their income, and in their reading-matter. Very little is translated into Albanian from newspapers and magazines, very few foreign magazines or books are allowed to enter the country, and the newspapers portray a land wholly united and virtually without problems. This is unfortunate, because everyone has a basic human right to his own opinion which, in a country of two and a half million, cannot be identical with everyone else's on all counts. And everybody has one or more kinds of problem.

The Albanian view, as expressed to me by the Editor of *Drita*, is that national unity must come before the wishes of the individual. Hoardings all over the country defy foreign 'blockades' and 'pressures', exalting Albanianism as the faith which will stimulate the nation to greater successes. Are these blockades and pressures imaginary, devised to excuse shortcomings in progress and to bolster the prevailing xenophobia? Or are they real, resulting from actions by the Western bloc ('imperialists' and 'capitalists' in Albanian terminology) and the Eastern bloc ('revisionists')?

The view from Albania looks very different from the view we have outside. Comrade Enver is convinced that the world is trying to subvert the Albanian way of life by every known means from economic sabotage to mini-skirts and popular music. The Yugoslavs, Soviets, and mainland Chinese are convinced that friendly overtures and aid were suspected and eventually spurned without good reason.

It may be that the truth lies, as usual, somewhere in between: that Comrade Enver and the Party of Labour of Albania have requested financial aid and diplomatic support on condition that their Stalinist interpretation of Marxist-Leninist theory and practice should not be contaminated, whereas successive allies, trying to reconcile principle with pragmatism, have moved away from a Stalinist line. Indeed, nowhere but in Albania can one still see conspicuous busts and life-size statues of Stalin in town centres.

The reason is that, despite the revelations of Stalin's grim record for brutality and large-scale inhumanity (perpetuated in each successive regime, according to Robert Conquest's *The Great Terror* and *The Gulag Archipelago* of Solzhenitsyn), Comrade Enver was treated by Stalin with paternal benevolence and his paternalistic attitude to the Albanian people owes much to Stalin's attitude to his own people. In *With Stalin* (1979), his memoirs of meetings with his early mentor, Comrade Enver stated: 'The ideological and cultural level of our party workers is low, but there is great eagerness to learn'. In earlier talks (July 1947), Stalin had enquired about the opposition to Communism in Albania. He was told: 'We have struck and continue to strike hard at internal reaction. We have had successes in our struggle to expose and defeat it. As for the physical liquidation of enemies, this has been done either in the direct clashes of our forces with the bands of armed criminals, or according to verdicts of people's courts in the trials of traitors and the closest collaborators of the occupiers. Despite the successes achieved, we still cannot say that internal reaction is no longer active.' This was in 1947, but the mysterious death of Albania's second most powerful man, Mehmet Shehu, late in 1981, is some indication that 'internal reaction' may persist.

Earlier still, Stalin had overlooked Albania altogether when secretly partitioning Europe between the capitalist and communist spheres of influence. He simply forgot it existed, both at the meeting with Churchill in Moscow (October 1944) and at the Yalta discussions with Churchill and Roosevelt (February 1945), when it was agreed that Greece would fall within Britain's sphere of influence, Romania within the Soviet sphere, and Hungary and Yugoslavia would be 'divided' equally, like sausages on a dinner table.

Later, in discussions held in Moscow with Dimitrov, Djilas and Kardelj, Stalin dismissed Dimitrov's concept of an East European Federation of nation-states, but recommended the establishment of a lesser union between Bulgaria and Romania, which should later 'incorporate' Albania. Not much about these talks is to be found in Comrade Enver's *With Stalin*.

8
Korçë and the Highlands

Though the eastern highlands of Albania comprise two-thirds of the nation's land-mass, for several reasons the average visitor will spend much less of his time there than in the more populous lowlands. First of all, longer distances and poor roads make longer days of travel and therefore shorter rest periods. Secondly, tourism facilities are in even shorter supply than in the coastal belt, the climate lending itself to comfortable travel only during the warmer summer months. And thirdly, slow and difficult agricultural and industrial development in the isolated village communities offers few opportunities for even the most ingenious propaganda.

It is in the mountains that the essential inwardness of Albanian life becomes most apparent. Taciturn shepherds, and a lonely widow at a cottage doorway, a boy throwing stones into a stream, a peasant turning, startled at our coach's roar, from his hoeing in a vegetable patch.

There are no regular tourist arrangements for Theth and the Albanian Alps on the northern border with Yugoslavia, but Albanians go there for winter sports, in the shadow of Mount Jezercë (2693m.). This is the zone of Bajram Curri and of the country's major hydro-electric station at Fierzë, with a power of 500,000 kilowatts, compared with the 620 kilowatts of the country's first (pre-Communist) station at Vithkuq near Korçë, and the 5,000 kilowatts of the first Communist-era 'Lenin' station near Tirana. Now every village in Albania possesses electric light, and the town of Fierzë, with its great dam 168m. high, employs six thousand workers.

Most visitors entering the Albanian mountains will do so from Tirana, by way of Elbasan. From Elbasan there is a run of 86km. to Pogradec and a further 40km. to Korçë. As far as Pogradec we follow roughly the route of the classical Via Egnatia, via Labinot and Librazhd. At Labinot a museum celebrates the National Conference which elected the Central Committee of the (then) Communist Party of Albania, with Comrade Enver Hoxha its first Secretary-General. Librazhd has recently added to its attractions standardised workers' apartment blocks to change its ancient character of ramshackle individualism. Most of Librazhd's workers are employed in bottling alcoholic drinks and different types of jam.

Still following the river Shkumbin, and the railway line, the coach passes Qukës on the right, then Prrenjas on the left. After crossing the high pass known as Qafë e Thanës—often blocked by snow in winter—the road descends sharply to Lin, where we first see Lake Ohrid, with a surface area of 360 sq.km. The lake could hardly be more different from Lake Shkodër in the north. The latter is barely above sea-level, for the most part extremely shallow, and for the most part unhealthy and muddy. Lake Ohrid is 700m. above sea-level, up to 286m. deep, and glitteringly pure and clear.

Lin is worth a stop, if you can prevail on your good Albturist driver and guide, for the sixth-century Byzantine basilica with its excellent mosaics in a good state of preservation in naves, chapels and baptistery. A long inscription in the narthex has been preserved almost intact due to the permanence of mosaic. The Lin mosaics are memorable for the symbolism of the vine, the birds, and—regrettably in a poor state of preservation—an asymmetrical masterpiece in the central nave representing the aquatic fauna of Lake Ohrid. My own idiosyncratic choice would be the portrait of a bee as if seen from above: possibly the earliest surviving bee in European art.

Pogradec

'Pogradec' is a form of the Slavic for 'at the foot of the castle', the castle in question being a fort built by Illyrians and strengthened in the Middle Ages. Some ruined walls have in fact been identified on a hill quite recently, justifying the name given by invading Bulgars to supersede the ancient name Encheleana. White sands on the lakeshore and the cleanliness of the pretty town give Pogradec an enviable reputation as a resort, with bracing mountain air and the serenity that only lakes bestow. Even the cows bathe in Lake Ohrid. Trout, carp, and eels are caught for local consumption in the Albturist hotel on the shore and for dispatch to Tirana, while fruit and vegetables comprise the major land crops. Artisans are involved with furniture design and manufacture, while as regards industry Pogradec can boast coalmines and a thriving chrome industry nearly rivalling that of Batra in the Martanesh highlands. Altogether, it is disappointing that the Albanian tourist authorities do not make more of the amenities of Pogradec, encouraging use of the eastern frontier with Yugoslavia.

Paul Edmonds left us a brief account of his experiences in Pogradec in

To the Land of the Eagle (1927). He made the acquaintance of the schoolmaster and the doctor. 'The doctor, who also ran the chemist's shop, as is customary in these parts, was cheery a little man bursting with local patriotism... He praised the water, the air, the scenery. He took me up a hill in the rear of the town and showed me the view. "Is there anywhere in the world a finer prospect than this?" he demanded. The local wine, he assured me, was as good as the best vintage champagne. And as for the climate—consumptives in the last stages of the disease begin to put on weight on the third day after their arrival, and what greater proof of its value could one have?

The inhabitants, although poor, were strong and healthy, and had many children (I did not need the doctor to tell me this, for children swarmed there), and altogether Pogradec was a paradise but for one thing—the lack of money. For the moment the worthy man overlooked the fact that this made the analogy all the closer'. Incidentally, Paul Edmonds stayed at the Hotel Continental in Tirana, and at the Hotel Europa in Shkodër (then known in its Italian form, Scutari), making his first flight ever on the Aero-Lloyd Line (subsidised by the German Government) from Tirana to Shkodër. The journey took forty minutes, as opposed to six hours by car, and was the last leg of a scheduled flight which started from Korçë and reached Tirana via Vlorë.

The route from Pogradec to Korçë crosses a plain between Lake Ohrid and Maliq. You should persuade your hosts to permit a visit to the recent excavations at Maliq, which are probably the major archaeological achievement since the last foreign team left. Maliq swamp has been cleared to create an impressive new state farm of 13,000 hectares, of which roughly half had been true swamp, and half useable but poor land now improved. The farm specialises in grain. The village of Maliq was founded in 1951 to serve the new sugar factory.

While draining the swamp in 1948 the workers encountered a variety of potsherds, and enough tools of flint and bone to convince them that the site was of more than purely local interest. During six consecutive seasons a team of archaeologists from Tirana identified strata inhabited from the Late Neolithic (in Albania this signifies the first half of the 3rd millennium B.C.) to the Late Bronze Age (the late 2nd millennium B.C.). The most striking evidence now exposed consists of hundreds of wooden piles driven into the swamp bed to provide foundations for rectangular reed huts whose walls were plastered with mud and straw. Copper axes and tools of stone and bone, found in abundance, can now be viewed in the museums at Korçë and Tirana. During the Bronze Age the water level sank to the point where huts could be built safely on the ground, without fear of wintry inundation. Look for spinning-wheel axles, fishnet weights, and those schematic terra cotta statuettes of women known in some parts of the Mediterranean as mother goddesses, or fertility figures, here not steatopygous as in the Willendorf figure or the reclining goddesses of Maltese prehistory, but deliciously slender.

Korçë

Korçë ('Gorica' is a Slavic word meaning 'small town') is the classical Pelium, recorded as having furnished supplies to the Roman army under Sulpicius in 200 B.C. Thereafter, the mountain town flits in and out of history until the late fifteenth century, when a mosque and public baths were built there by Hodja (in Albanian spelling 'Hoxha') Elias Bey, who had taken part in the siege and capture of Constantinople by the Ottoman armies in 1453. Korçë continued its steady growth as a commercial and crafts centre, with a name for rugs and carpets. A stronghold of the Orthodox Christianity, Korçë possessed a church in 898 which was rebuilt in 1391.

Many local people emigrated to the U.S.A., Egypt and Romania early in the twentieth century, and the anguished, strife-torn history of Korçë in the last hundred years can stand as a paradigm for the suffering of the Albanian people under successive regimes. The Greeks occupied the town, which is so near their border, on 6 December 1912, then in 1915 the French—also operating from Greek territory (Thessaloniki)—established an independent 'Republic of Koritza' which issued its own banknotes until the French retired on 21 June 1920. Communist martyrs of Korçë include Ali Kelmendi (trained in Moscow); Koci Bako, who fell victim of the Fascist occupation forces during a demonstration on 8 November 1941, the day when the Albanian Communist Party was founded; and seventy others killed during a demonstration in 1943.

Apart from the local Archaeological Museum, Korçë possesses an interesting Museum of Education to commemorate the fact that in this building the first Albanian-language school was founded in 1887; a High School with French as the medium of instruction was opened in 1917. If you are surprised at the generously-proportioned mansions dating for the most part to the years before World War II, remember that many emigrants not only sent enough money back home for their daughters' dowries and their sons' education, but also saved enough to build a comfortable home for their own retirement years. Hence the mixture of the neo-classical and baroque which seem to suggest a Nash terrace surrounding Sant' Ivo alla Sapienza. Odd, of course, but certainly amusing and in a strange way touching.

To serve the artistic interests of a town of 50,000 which many tacitly take for the cultural capital of Albania there is an Art Gallery (in the former home of the landscape-painter Vangjush Mio), a theatre named for the poet A.Z. Çajupi, a variety theatre, a local radio station, and a Palace of Culture. Which leads one to enquire why, in a state devoted to workers, one should call a meeting-place a Palace of Culture, when a Cottage or House of Culture might sound less aristocratically pretentious. A new stadium and swimming-pool offer the local sportsman excellent facilities.

Albturist may arrange for you a visit to the Carpet Factory, which employs almost exclusively women and young girls. These weavers work 8 hours a day, six days a week, on handwoven carpets to Persian designs at 360,000 knots to the square metre!

From the belvedere overlooking the town you can gain a good impression of the town, and its surrounding plains and villages. Try to get out to the nearby village of Mborjë to see the Byzantine Church of the Ascension (1389), with frescoes internal and external. Though heavily restored, the Dormition of the Virgin hints at notable original quality, in the admittedly narrow aesthetic confines of Byzantine art.

But the best Byzantine painting in this area is to be found at the Church of St Nicholas (Kisha e Shën Kollit) constructed in 1726 at Voskopojë, 24km. west of Korçë. The name is a corruption of the Greek 'Moskhopolis', meaning calf-city. Voskopojë is known to have existed in the fourteenth century, but it was not until the 18th century that its cultural apogee was reached, with an Albanian-language printing press, library, scriptorium, and a community of painters such as David of Selenicë and the brothers Constantinos and Athanasios. Of the many churches and monasteries of Voskopojë, nowadays only seven survive, and we can see only Shën Koll and the ruined monastery of Shën Prodhom, the latter with a few frescoes saved from the devastation attributed first to Ali Pasha of Tepelenë and Ibrahim Pasha of Berat, and finally to the occupying Fascists.

The lively, even exuberant realism of David's 'Crucifixion of St Peter' is probably the finest achievement at Shën Koll, which is almost entirely David's own work, with some help from his assistants Christos and Constantinos. But many prefer the first true portrait ever painted in Albania: that of Haxhi Jorgji, with wise, almost humorous eyes, a generous, decorous moustache and flowing beard. And if the nose is full of character, and the temple aged with grace, few would deny that it is the hands which render the figure fully human, solidly fleshy and articulated as no Byzantine artist in Albania had dared before. The irreal landscape behind Christ as he heals the blind looks back to the genesis of Byzantine art, while the donor Haxhi Jorgji looks towards its apotheosis.

The great apsidal frescoes surviving here, so far not only from Tirana, but even from the mountain roads that link Korçë with Ersekë and Pogradec, are flanked by local costumes and local saints, such as St Nicomedes of Vithkuq and the composer-saint John Coucouzelis. A Greek mountain flautist plays at the birth of Christ much as a Vlach shepherd in the hills around Voskopojë will play the flute today.

Kukës

Since Albturist opened in 1982 tourist mountain routes to Kukës (2 days @ £15.75) and to Burrel and Peshkopi (2 days @ £15.45), I am appending notes on these, since you will find nothing in the current official Albturist literature: their most recent guidebook is in any case dated 1969, and has been out of print for many years.

Kukës, the classical Gubuleum, is normally reached from Durrës or Tirana on the highway through Laç and the Mirditë hill region, or from Shkodër via Pukë. The two roads merge just east of Pukë, which is 56km. east of Shkodër, and from there the run is hilly, winding, and perpetually fascinating, with always the chance of meeting wolves and bears. The country is agriculturally poor, but isolated hamlets and mountain cottages are occasionally glimpsed beside the road, or on a slope affording just enough soil for a vegetable patch. Goats graze with a hint of desperation lest night descend before they have devoured enough to keep them alive till morning. After another 38km. we are at the summit of Qafë e Malit—a mountain pass whose name officially means 'mountain pass', though there are thousands such, and in 47km., having passed numerous hairpin bends and the tiny villages of Vrrith, Shëmri, Barbçorët and Kolsh, we emerge into the new town of Kukës. The old village of Kukës has disappeared below the waters of Fierzë's lake, and the new centre is barely twenty years old, its workers being for the most part employed in the copper mines. Copper accounted for 2% of national industrial production in 1950, 0.7% in 1960, 4.7% in 1970, and 4.3% in 1979, according to *35 Vjet Shqipëri Socialiste* (1979).

The World Bank indicated that national product per head in Albania was US$40 in 1979, the lowest in Europe and only one third that of neighbouring Yugoslavia. Reliance on only one major partner (Yugoslavia from 1944 to 1948; the U.S.S.R. to 1961; and the People's Republic of China to 1977) and subsequent 'self-reliance' has led to such economic backwardness that only a narrow view of ideological purity can justify further steps in the same direction. The effect of Albania's ideological straitjacket has been to retard the creation of infrastructure such as adequate roads and new industries, encumber their expansion once formed, and delay the introduction of fully mechanised agriculture and automated industry. Though the rail link north to Shkodër was inaugurated in November 1981, there is no sign of the promised extension to the border post of Han i Hotit (and south from Titograd on the Yugoslav side) which would link Albania to the European rail network. Neither is there as much air traffic as in the 1930s, when Aero-Lloyd, financed by a German company, was succeeded by the Italian-run Ala Littoria, connecting Tirana with Shkodër, Durrës, Vlorë, Gjirokastër, Korçë and Kukës. The introverted, xenophobic attitudes which have persuaded Comrade Enver never to give an interview to a foreign journalist, and which restrict visits abroad by Albanians, naturally militate against economic development and trade.

It is undoubtedly here in the north that the majority of health problems are found. An official report (1968–9) summarising a study of 1,580 children up to three years old sampled across thirteen northern districts showed that as many as 60% were suffering from neuromuscular disorders, and 47% from rickets. The Government attributed these figures to malnutrition and unsatisfactory sanitary and hygienic arrangements in their homes, but it is probable that some improvements have been made in the last decade. In 1980 it was stated that Albania had 1 doctor for every 579 citizens. The average life expectancy was 69 years.

Burrel

To reach Burrel and Peshkopi from Durrës or Tirana, one would take the good road as far as Krujë, then the inferior road east, over the Qafë e Shtambës, 1230m. above sea-level. Burrel, centre of the Mat district, is 37km. from Krujë, and though the town, formerly Muslim, is small, it presents important insights into typical manners and customs of the mountain-dwelling Albanians of the north, who are still to some extent governed by the unwritten law of Lek Dukagjin, or simply 'Lek'. The standard work on the *Kanun*, or law, of Lek is *The Unwritten Law of Albania* (1954) by Margaret Hasluck, an Englishwoman who lived for several years in Elbasan.

The law of Lek covers inheritance and crime, especially murder, bodily assault, and theft. It seems to derive from a certain Alexander ('Lek') Dukagjin, Lord of Dagno and Zadrima (1444–59) who fled with others to Italy in 1479 when the Turks captured Shkodër, returning after the death of Sultan Mehmet II in 1481. Apparently a Christian, Lek was nevertheless excommunicated by Pope Paolo II in 1464 for his 'most un-Christian code' or Canon of Laws. Since Lek is ignored thereafter by most Christian writers, and nowadays by Communists rightly repudiating the blood feud, it might be useful to recapitulate some of the ordinances by which Lek sought to prescribe and enforce punishment for crime in the northern Albanian highlands.

Crime was checked by the prescription of specific punishments, and enforced by a council of tribal elders. Fines and house-burning became alternatives in retribution to the automatic death-penalty. Vendetta (so-called from Sicily) or blood-feud could quickly have degenerated into mass extermination without a code of honour to which all males had to subscribe (there was no blood-feud affecting women, protected either alone or escorted by menfolk).

Like Sicilians (among whom many of them settled), mountain-dwelling Albanians have a peculiar sensitivity to a perceived affront, whether by physical blow, verbal insult, or even dispute on a matter of fact. Wounding was merely fined according to the degree of injury; in the case of proven accidental injury, the aggressor's house was not burnt down. Murder beyond the tribe was avenged by any male relative on any male relative of the murderer, a chain which continued until stopped by both tribal councils. Murder within the tribe was much more common, due to daily proximity, and the rules consequently more complex. The killer tried to escape to a house beyond the tribe, where he had to be given hospitality; his male relatives also tried to escape, if they were prudent. The killer's wife and children, sisters and aunts, were forced to scatter into other homes, where they had to be accepted. Then the council of elders ordered the killer's house and chattels to be burnt, and might also destroy his animals and devastate his lands. The murderer could ask the council for a *besa*, or truce. If granted, elders were appointed by the murderer and the Lord of Blood (Zot i Gjakut) of the Council of Elders, to explore the facts, reach a just settlement, and ensure that it was sworn in the local church or mosque. A permanent *besa* between families or tribes was effected by a ritual of blood-brotherhood, or by a marriage alliance. Killing was not punishable for adultery or rape, or if a murderer was sought out and killed the same day.

After the monotonous military architecture of defensive concrete bunkers beside every crossroad, and commanding every hilltop and mountain pass, every hamlet and every plain, it is refreshing to come across the traditional domestic architecture of the northern *kullë* ('tower'). The multi-storeyed towers preceded jerry-built apartment blocks for families transplanted to run farms and factories, but what they lack in egalitarian facelessness they make up for in character, stolidity, and strength.

Around Burrel and the mouth of the river Mat, semi-nomads once used to winter on the swampy plains in houses which, in the words of Margaret Hasluck, 'had walls of planking or wattle and daub, with roofs of tiles or strips of wood. They rested on vertical sections of tree trunks about two feet high which had been laid at close intervals on the ground but had not been driven into like piles. In this way they kept snug and dry even during the winter floods. All over Albania granaries were raised some distance from the ground in order to keep out the rats, but so far as is known, there were no houses on stilts except at the mouth of the Mat'—to which one now has to add archaeological data from Maliq near Korçë, as revealed earlier in this chapter.

The *kullë* began as a simple two-roomed house (sitting-room and kitchen), to which the father added one room at a time as each of his married sons brought a bride back home, to a height of two, three or even four storeys. A home built laterally around the original nucleus, instead of vertically, was known as a *shtëpi* (from the Latin *hospitium*, 'guest-chamber, lodging'). A *shtëpi* too could have more than one storey, in which case the interior staircase was fixed. The *kullë*, a house-type normally preferred in isolated mountain areas where vendetta was endemic, possessed between one floor and the next an inner ladder that could be instantly drawn up at the first threat of violent intrusion; trapdoors over staircase and ladder could be instantly slammed shut in case of need. In a *kullë*, livestock, farm tools, and such fodder as hay could be protected from thieves on the ground floor, whereas in a *shtëpi* they were put in sheds in the yard.

Segregation of the sexes, practised by Albanian Muslims, Roman Catholics, and Orthodox Christians alike, meant that the menfolk assembled in the sitting-room, and women folk in the (often draughty) kitchen.

Security being paramount, there were often no windows on the ground floor, tiny openings being smaller than any young boy could squeeze through, and higher than even the tallest man could look through. Some square or rectangular holes for ventilation and light were left in the upper floors of the *kullë*, but at night they were sealed with stone slabs, or wooden shutters. The hearth in the kitchen was set in the middle, so that everyone could obtain equal benefit from the warmth.

If we find the *kullë* or *shtëpi* ruggedly charming or picturesque, let us never fall into the trap of believing that such was the intention. If they are grouped together like a honeycomb, it is for mutual protection. If they are strung along a hill ridge, it is for observation. If they are set in a lush green valley, it is because of easy access to water, and good grazing.

An Albanian's identification with his own plot of land was so absolute, until Communist collectivization was imposed, that descendants of a family which had emigrated a hundred years earlier might return to claim title to house and land, removing any squatters from their property. Even if an emigrant sold his land before departure 'together with all that is on it', the actual site of the house remained his in spite of the contract of sale, and no-one might use that site for building. (In Mirditë there was a fixed term of only ten years, however, and a settler could occupy his house thereafter). Before compulsory collectivization, the Albanian peasant owned his house and land, and cared nothing for rent or eviction. His village and tribe owning forest and grazing-grounds, he could fetch firewood and graze his sheep there at will. He could sell animals for cash to buy tobacco, coffee, sugar, clothing, brides for his sons, and to pay taxes. A man could work as hard as he liked, and reap the reward of his own labours, or laze away at subsistence level, working only when he felt like it. This choice—this human freedom—has vanished, and who is to say that its disappearance has tended to the common good?

Peshkopi

Travelling east from Burrel 43km. to Peshkopi one crosses the Black Drin after passing between the Dejë and Allaman mountains. Dibër was the

Peshkopi, 1943.

capital of the Albanian administrative district of Dibra until 1926, when the town became Yugoslav after changes in the international frontiers. Now the capital of Dibra-in-Albania is Peshkopi, the Albanian form of the classical 'Episcopi', denoting the presence of an early bishopric. The rambling town is built on the side of a hill slope, its historic centre being surrounded by two- and three-storey buildings. Invigorating mountain air is one good reason for choosing the Albturist route to Peshkopi and the Dibra highlands: another is the spectacular drive through valleys and woods still almost unspoilt by the raucous voice and garish hand of the twentieth century. This is walking country, rambling country, thinking country: for the botanist and solitary ornithologist.

With Peshkopi, the latest addition to Albania's list of towns which may be visited by foreigners, we finish touring Albania. But since we are in collective-land, let us leave the last words not to the author, but to the rest of the group, as they were asked their opinions for the record on the Titograd side of the border.

'It was a tremendous experience, and in a strange way lived up to the strangest of my expectations, but I don't think I should like to go back.'

'Definitely the most interesting country in Eastern Europe.'

'I came for the beaches, and was bored by the endless propaganda.'

'We'd like to come again and see all the places that we had to miss on this visit.'

'It's a great shame that the Albanians know so little of the outside world and care even less to learn anything.'

'The archaeology was my motive for visiting Albania, and there is clearly very much more to do, since it is so low on their list of priorities.'

'The progress that has been made astonished me, when I saw pictures of what conditions used to be like.'

'The personality cult of Hoxha, and the survival here of Stalin's statues that have been pulled down even in the Soviet Union, probably surprised me more than the obvious economic problems.'

'The countryside is so beautiful and unspoilt that it reminded us of Ireland before the Second World War and England before the First.'

'It's a pity you aren't allowed to drive your own car around Albania, because the distances are short, and the hotels quite adequate, but on a bus tour you spend a great deal of time just waiting around.'

'Yes, I'd come again: it's so very strange that I think you would need a number of visits to get to know the country and people really well.'

Useful Information

When to Come — How to Come — Tours and Excursions — Hotels and Restaurants—Passports and Visas—Customs, Currency, Immigration—Luggage and Clothing—Shopping—Communications—Health—Diplomatic Representation—Speaking the Language—Words and Phrases—Numbers—Days and Months—Official Holidays and Festivals—Books and Maps

When to Come

The true traveller, who explores new places for knowledge, beauty, and enlightenment, will prefer Spring (April, May) or Autumn (October, November) to visit Albania. Atheists can enjoy a non-Christmas there, while sunbathers in search of Mediterranean beaches at pre-war prices will stay in Durrës in June, July, and August, with a venture to Sarandë and Butrint. The mountains are to be visited from April to October, for preference: Winter there is cold to very cold, with heavy rainfall. Summer in the lowlands is warm to hot, with very scant rainfall. The district around Theth in the north is considered alpine, whereas the coastal zone south of Vlorë is considered Mediterranean. Consider the snow-capped Cedars of Lebanon cold above sun-swathed coastal Byblos, and you will get the idea. The average maximum lowland Summer day-temperature is 95°F: Shkodër 93.2°, Vlorë 104° and Durrës 91.4°. Nights are warm to very warm, with a July average of 77°. There is a regular sea breeze all along the coast, but northern Europeans might find the heat (and sometimes also the humidity) quite oppressive. A siesta after lunch is recommended, and generally provided on tours.

Winter is mild on the coast, with a January average of 47°F at Durrës and 48° at Vlorë, but much colder inland: Berat 43°, Tirana 42°, Elbasan 41°. Frosts occur in January, and snow may lie for some time on higher ground inland.

Rainfall is generally heaviest in November and March, though Vlorë experiences 62% of its rainfall and Shkodër 50% in September, and Durrës 50% in December. There is virtually no rain at all from June to August, extending to October on the coast. Heavy Winter rains often disrupt transport, making many of the bad minor roads impassable.

Regent Holidays, Small St., Bristol, operate tours from Britain all the year round, with an emphasis on the warmer months, on behalf of Albturist, Bulevardi Deshmorët e Kombit 6, Tirana.

How to Come

From the U.K. one will enter Albania by land across the border between Titograd (Yugoslavia) and Shkodër. It would be delightful to be able to fly in from Heathrow to Tirana, or to sail in the three miles from Corfu to Sarandë. But until the authorities allow liberal entry to the country, including an individual visa, hiking, camping and caravanning, a permit to bring in one's own car, and allowing Mediterranean cruise liners to call at Durrës for a stop-over, one will just have to conform to the Regent Holidays booking arrangements.

Diplomatic relations between France and Albania are currently more amicable than those between Great Britain and Albania, so if you speak French you may prefer to go with Trans-Tours, 49 Avenue de l'Opéra, Paris 1. There is a non-stop Paris-Tirana flight by Pakistan International Airlines once a week, and a Rome-Tirana flight once a week via Bari by Alitalia, and Rome-Tirana-Bucharest by Tarom. Though arrangements can change at any time, at present there are also three flights a week to Tirana from Belgrade on JAT, one from Bucharest on MALEV, and one from Athens on Olympic. Interflug (G.D.R.) operates a service from Tirana to East Berlin.

Tours and Excursions

Regent Holidays tours to Albania start in April and end early in January. The shortest six last ten days (all based in Tirana) and in 1982 cost from £265 to £275 plus insurance, group visa, and a small surcharge for increased hotel prices. Two Summer tours are based in Durrës, costing £280 for 13 days and £305 for 17. Undoubtedly the best value are the two general tours lasting two weeks in June and September at about £350. One can combine two lots of shorter tours giving 17 days in Albania for £415 or 20 for £425. City-based groups must pay extra for excursions but cannot be sure of getting on to any particular tour. Single-room supplements cost from £2.70 per night in the long low season to £3.50 per night between 28 July and 28 September.

Itineraries are fixed by Albturist often as late as the previous day, so Regent Holidays and their valiant couriers must not be blamed for last-minute alterations or disappointments beyond their control: and—as in China—*most* tour arrangements are beyond the U.K. agent's control.

Only a few of the holidays offered in Albania consist of general tours: the majority consist of one-centre or two-centre holidays based in Tirana or Durrës, and individuals will book and pay for their own tours for the following day, departing at 8 a.m. unless otherwise indicated, breakfast being served from 7. As tours are planned to return to your hotel by 6.30 p.m., there is always time to book the excursion for the following day before the Albturist representative in the hotel leaves at 7. I have given sample prices of excursions from Durrës in 1982 prices expressed in leks @ 12.5 leks to £1.

Half-day tours leave from Durrës hotels at 9 a.m. for a pioneer camp (6 leks), Durrës town (13 leks), and Kavajë town (22 leks); a half-day tour leaves for a state farm at 4 p.m. (18 leks).

Excursions from Durrës lasting one day or more are listed below. Prices from Tirana are similar. It must be emphasised that most tours will only be arranged for a minimum of fifteen persons, and these may often be from a variety of nationalities.

To	Days	Price in leks
Tirana	1	43
Tirana and Krujë	1	49
·· ·· ··	2	155
Krujë ·	1	38
··	2	120
Berat	1	62
Berat, Fier and Apollonia	1	85
·· ·· ·· ··	2	184
Fier and Apollonia	1	65
Fier and Vlorë	1	42
·· ·· ··	2	178
·· ·· ·· and Berat	2	182
Vlorë	1	79
··	2	165
Lezhë	1	56
Lezhë and Shkodër	1	86
·· ·· ··	2	173
Shkodër	1	82
··	2	169
Shkodër and Krujë	1	90
·· ·· ··	2	176
·· ·· ·· and Lezhë	1	92
·· ·· ·· ·· ··	2	178
Elbasan and Tirana	1	68
·· ·· ··	2	153
Elbasan, Pogradec and Korçë	2	218
·· ·· ·· ··	3	304

To	Days	Price in leks
Gjirokastër, Sarandë and Fier	3	306
Gjirokastër and Fier	2	193
Fier, Gjirokastër and Sarandë	2	235
.. ..	4	392
.. .. and Vlorë	4	381
Fier, Berat, Apollonia, Sarandë and Vlorë	4	401
Kukës	2	195
Burrel and Peshkopi	2	191

Hotels and Restaurants

Since there is no choice of hotels, the visitor simply needs to be told what to expect.

In Tirana, British groups usually go to the Hotel Tirana on Skanderbeg Square, the city centre. Facilities are first class, if not de luxe, and all bedrooms have a private shower or bath. Ask for a view of the square, which is fascinating at night when the *passeggiata* takes over from the officious traffic police who are reduced to whistling angrily at pedestrians, in the absence of traffic. The alternative hotel in Tirana is the Italian-built Dajti, also very near the city centre.

In Durrës you may be lucky and stay at the Hotel Adriatiku, but at the height of Summer it is usual for groups to stay at the Apollonia, Durrësi or Butrinti, which are all one grade lower. They all have hot and cold running water, and some rooms have a private shower. For the rest, waylay a chambermaid and beg her to unlock one of the public showers on each floor: that is, if you can find a chambermaid. Some are so reluctant to let you shower that it seems they must fear rape.

Visitors generally rated the Hotel Çajupi in Gjirokastër, Tomori in Berat, and Butrinti in Sarandë fairly high, and the Rozafat in Shkodër, Skampa in Elbasan, and Apollonia in Fier rather low, but it must be stressed that there is no choice, and you must put up with small rooms, erratic plumbing, and possibly perilous electrical fittings with foresight and equanimity. Take a little doggy rubber ball as an all-purpose plug for bath, shower and wash-basin, since plugs are not a feature of contemporary Albanian life. Though the odd single room can occasionally be provided, it cannot be guaranteed throughout a trip: everyone must be prepared to share a room, singles with someone of the same sex.

Elsewhere, reasonable hotels are to be found in Lezhë and Vlorë in the lowlands, and Pogradec and Korçë in the mountains.

Be very careful to dispose of *everything* you want to throw away in the waste-paper basket, because after you leave a systematic search is made in your room to ensure you have left nothing behind. On the first days of every tour, the coach is delayed as frantic maids rush into the bus with empty Kleenex boxes, used razor blades, and other objects you had rather hoped would not be held up to the amusement of fellow-travellers. One tourist remarked how fanatically honest the maids were. Another commented on the likely consequences of their being found to have kept anything they found in a guest bedroom.

One eats almost all meals in hotel restaurants, and as these are substantial and often lengthy affairs, there is little opportunity (as indeed is the intention) for tourists to mingle with Albanians in cafés, the odd *byrektore* (pie-shop, selling meat and cheese pies) or the *akullore* (ice-cream parlour), where good children are taken for a treat.

A translation of a typical menu may be of interest, since (apart from dietary requirements made clear beforehand) there is no choice and hence no written menu on any tourist table in Albanian hotels: if you found one, it would be in Albanian. So here is an indication of what you could have chosen for lunch or dinner at the Hotel Butrinti, Sarandë, one day in June 1982, with weight in grammes and prices in leks @ £0.8½ per lek:

Mixed hors d'oeuvres	250	6.20
Tomato salad	220	1.40
Salad with olives	200	2.20
Mixed salad with gherkins	165	2.20
Vegetable soup	250	2.30
Meat risotto	300	4.90
Maccheroni with meat	330	4.20
Maccheroni with sauce	330	3.10
Maccheroni with butter	300	3.10
Fried fish	330	5.90
Veal balls with vegetables	300	6.70
Grilled veal with vegetables	250	6.40
Veal with potatoes	300	6.60
Scotch eggs	200	5.60
Chicken with vegetables	310	7.80
Chicken with potatoes	300	7.90
Veal roll with vegetables	300	7.00
Mixed vegetables (without meat)	250	2.40

National Dishes

Goulash	250	2.80
Meat and yoghourt	200	6.50

Korçë meat balls	340	7.00
White cheese	100	2.70
Kaçkavallë cheese	95	4.30

Desserts

Cherries	250	2.00
Fruit cocktail	200	2.00
Cream cake	80	3.50
Creme caramel	250	3.10

Drinks

Korçë beer	bottle	3.00
Red or white Riesling	250	2.00
Përmeti raki 18°	50	2.50
Ouzo	50	3.00
'Glina' mineral water	bottle	2.00

The average tourist lunch is of four courses, beginning with soup for example, then possibly maccheroni, meat, or fish with plentiful vegetables, and for dessert a cream cake or fruit in season or both. One takes a coffee or liqueur in the bar, where the charge is extra. Natural water is not recommended with meals: the excellent mineral water (Uji Glina) so-called from the spring near Gjirokastër costs 17 pence a litre. Ample red and white wines are available, as are such confections as orangeade and lemonade, but fruit juices are found only intermittently, while Coca Cola and its kin are banned.

Dinner normally comprises three courses, and is served about 7.30. Salad is always served, and is invariably fresh.

Breakfast varies from the substantial, with omelette, and jam and fresh rolls, to the unsatisfactory, with stale bread and jam. Coffee may not always be obtainable at breakfast: tea may not always be served with milk, and the milk generally leaves much to be desired. Sugar too is poor in quality, like the salt.

The quality of the cooking is almost invariably good, more varied than its reputation abroad will allow, though it sometimes lacks the last nuance of subtlety. Over a holiday of some three hundred and fifty guest days, totalling a thousand meals and more, there were only four cases reported of indigestion or worse: an almost complete vindication of Albanian cooking.

Passports and Visas

Your passport must be current for the entire duration of your stay in

Albania. A group visa will then be obtained on your behalf when you return your visa application (currently £6.80) with four passport-style photographs. Your details on the visa form must correspond *exactly* with the details in your passport. You keep the passport, and your courier will keep the group visa. You will need to hand your passport in at each hotel reception desk for registration when receiving your room key; remember to ask for your passport back when handing over the room key on departure, or before going to a bank to change money.

Customs, Currency, Immigration

Do not attempt to bring in any Bible or Quran or other religious literature even for your own use: not only will it be confiscated, but you will be suspected of illegal missionary activity and deported immediately. Similarly avoid bringing in any books or magazines that might be offensive to a maiden aunt. Ladies with mini or maxi dresses will be asked to change; men with full beard of long hair will be asked to visit the barber. All possessions such as watches, cameras, tape recorders and suchlike must be registered both on arrival and departure, to ensure you have not disposed of them en route.

Albanian coins are 5, 10, 20, 50 qindarkas and 1 lek; notes are issued in denominations of 1 lek, 3, 5, 10, 25, 50 and 100. 100 qindarkas = 1 lek.

Do not try to import or export Albanian leks; any small change you have left on the last day can be spent on drink, cigarettes, matches, or gifts in Shkodër. Large quantities of leks should be changed in Tirana or Durrës on your last day before departure: allow plenty of time for lengthy procedures at the foreign exchange counter. Some hotel-shops accept only leks, and others only hard currency. Some of them price in US$, which they will convert into sterling; yet others price in leks and require leks. You may be asked to accept change for sterling in any hard currency. At present the lek is 12.5 to the £1, but of course this will change.

Do not tip with money. You can give cigarettes to the driver, stockings or books to your courier.

For your two nights in Yugoslavia you may wish to take in dinars, which may be bought in small quantities at your local U.K. bank before departure and changed on return. No visa is needed for U.K. visitors to Yugoslavia at present, but check the current situation.

Immigration formalities are very strict, and must be carefully adhered to, including walking through a puddle of disinfectant while crossing the Yugoslav border into Albania. There is no requirement for a vaccination certificate of any kind.

Luggage and Clothing

No assistance is given by hotel staff to visitors in the matter of taking suitcases from the bus to the hotel foyer to their room, so take lightweight cases and the minimum of luggage. The older generation will benefit from cases on wheels or trolleys.

Men will wear short-sleeved shirts and comfortable trousers or jeans in the Summer, with a pullover or jacket for evenings, but no tie. Women are advised to take several interchangeable long-sleeved blouses and skirts, with some lightweight but modest dresses. A hat or parasol is advised in the Summer; an umbrella in the Winter. Open sandals are best in Summer; comfortable walking shoes in Winter. Beachwear should be as decorous as possible, and confined to the beach. Even the best hotels in Tirana and Durrës do not suggest a tie or formal dress. Laundries are quick, cheap and efficient in long-stay hotels, but if you are planning one-night stands take washing-powder: hot water is available in your room almost everywhere, and clothes dry quickly in Summer. Electric supply is 220 volts.

Shopping

All shops are state-owned, so supplies of most goods are limited in quality and quantity. Carpets are relatively expensive (compared with food or drink) but make an excellent souvenir, as does the plain pottery (but not the garish glazed animals and costume ceramics).

Books are a first-rate souvenir, but must be posted by air from Tirana or Durrës before departure. Most are considered offensive by the Yugoslav authorities and hence confiscated by them. It will cost you less to buy a book in Albania and send it to the U.K. by air than to buy the same book in England. But if you cannot go to Albania, shop at The Albanian Shop, 3 Betterton St., London WC2H 9BP (open 12.30–18.00 Monday to Friday) or by post from The Albanian Society, 26 Cambridge Road, Ilford, Essex. The Albanian Shop sells Riza's attractive *Gjirokastra* album for £12.50 when the Albanian equivalent is £2.10, and The Albanian Society prices *The Social Class Structure of the Working Class in Albania* at £1.00 when the price in Albania is £0.28. Both outlets provide dependable, essential services and should be patronised. To pack your books in Albania, remember to take CushionWrap or brown paper and cardboard, Sellotape, scissors and string.

Silversmithing in all its various forms is still practised in Krujë and elsewhere, though craftsmanship has degenerated in recent years, and fine specimens are now hard to come by. Silk and cotton goods may attract you. Objects carved in wood include cigarette boxes and bowls.

Turkish delight and cognac make acceptable presents. Records and cassettes of folk music are on sale, and a shop selling musical instruments in Tirana may appeal to some visitors.

Local matches and cigarettes with party slogans and symbols are eye-catching, but I found it very difficult indeed to buy posters, and much more could be done in this direction in hotels. Some hotels offer a range of books and postcards, though even local newspapers are not found there. Even the biggest bookshops have a tiny selection of current Albanian magazines, and no foreign magazines whatsoever.

Shopping hours tend to be very variable, but you are most likely to catch a shop open between 9 and 12 a.m. and 4 and 7 p.m. Go to banks in the morning, and to post offices in morning or evening, except on the Adriatiku beach in Durrës, where the post office stays open 24 hours a day. Explore the Ma-Po (*Magazinë Popullor*) in each town for the range of consumer durables, and contrast it with the supermarket over the border in Titograd for range, price and quality. The *Ma-Pos* remind me of the Dickensian East End of London: dull colours, unsmiling shop assistants in drab smocks behind the barricade of their counter, and a depressing uniformity of goods. You are likelier to enjoy shopping more in Tirana (where the hotel is central) or in Gjirokastër (where the bazaar is endlessly fascinating, tiny shops ascending the cobbled streets on both sides), than in Durrës (where the hotel is miles from the shopping centre) or Elbasan.

Typical prices: glazed eagle 24 leks (@ 12.5 to £1), glazed girl in national costume 28 leks, glass flamingo 5 leks, glass flower vase a foot high 90 leks, carpet from Korçë 3207 leks (all in tourist's shop beside the open-air mosaics, centre of Sarandë), men's sandals 85 leks a pair, eggs 0.8 lek each, peas 1.3 leks per kg., 3 leks a large loaf (not wrapped, either in the shop or for the customer to take away), meat as available 15–17 leks per kg., plum jam 5.5 leks a jar, cotton shirt or blouse 70–100 leks, and a man's two-piece suit of poor quality 700 leks. Compare these prices with the average wage of 720 leks per month. Rents are deductible at 3% of one's salary. Direct taxes were abolished in 1969.

Communications

Send all postcards, letters, newspapers, magazines and books by *airmail*, since surface mail will go via Yugoslavia, and from time to time (including 1982) the Yugoslav authorities will confiscate any manuscript or printed material which they deem to be pro-Albanian and hence anti-Yugoslav.

Airmail from Albania arrives in five to fifteen days at U.K. addresses, and three heavy parcels of books sent airmail from the Durrës post office beside the Hotel Adriatiku cost me a total of 43 leks, about £3.40.

There are telephone links with other European countries, though it may take some time to contact the U.K. Ask for the number at the reception desk of your hotel, or at the post offices in Durrës, Tirana, and other main centres.

Since it is difficult to obtain telephone directories, it may be helpful to note some numbers you can dial from your room telephone in the Hotel Adriatiku, Durrës.

Switchboard 11	Reception, Hotel Apollonia 24
Hotel management 35	Reception, Hotel Kruja 37
Hotel service 36	Reception, Hotel Butrinti 38
Floor service 57	Reception, Hotel Durrësi 44
Accounts 33	Buffet 41
Reception 63	Patisserie 42
Information 31	Laundry 44

Health

A doctor will be called if necessary speedily and without charge. Military aircraft are available to take emergency cases to hospital, also without charge. The visitor pays only for prescriptions. However, it is *always* advisable to take out sufficient insurance cover (including medical, holiday cancellation, and baggage loss or damage), so that if you have to be flown home it can be arranged without financial hardship.

Diplomatic Representation

Albania has relations with some eighty foreign countries, but the United States of America and Great Britain are not of their number. Indeed no American citizen except Jack Shulman (Editor of *Albania Report*, P.O. Box 912, New York, N.Y. 10008) may enter Albania, and he has no official diplomatic status. Neither has William B. Bland, Secretary of the non-party organisation called The Albanian Society, 26 Cambridge Road, Ilford, Essex (tel. 01—590 9977), who is a source of information, books and magazines about Albania.

The nearest Albanian Embassy to the U.K. is that in France at 131 Rue de la Pompe, Paris 16e. (tel. 553 51—32).

The following nations are represented at ambassadorial level in Tirana: Bulgaria, People's Republic of China, Cuba, Czechoslovakia, Egypt, France, German Democratic Republic, Greece, Hungary, Italy, Democratic People's Republic of Korea, Poland, Romania, Turkey, Vietnam, and Yugoslavia.

British and Irish passport-holders do not need double-transit visas for

Yugoslavia, but at present British Commonwealth passport-holders do: these should be obtained from your nearest Yugoslav Consulate.

Speaking the Language

The Albanian Language is not only very beautiful, but is of absorbing interest for its complex genesis and evolution, which are still far from clear after a century of scholarly research. The consensus nowadays follows the belief of the Austrian philologist Gustav Meyer that the Indo-European tongue now called Albanian was a dialect of ancient Illyrian. Yet this adds up to little enough, for despite the additional investigation of Hans Krahe (1925 and 1929), we know so little about Illyrian, or Phrygo-Thracian as it has also been called. This is one of the few surviving sentences in Illyrian, which we can read, but not so far understand: *Klaohizis thotoria mar ta pi vastei basta veinan aran.* One of the mysteries of world language is why Albanian, so close to Greek and Latin, should have had no extant written literature earlier than the Liturgy of Don Gjon Buzuk internally dated 1554—5 and housed in the Vatican Library in Rome. The Gegs of Northern Albania and the Tosks of the south have had their own dialects. Stuart Mann's *Short Albanian Grammar* (1932) was based on Geg, but standard literary Albanian is now based on Tosk, and Mann's grammar has been replaced by *Standard Albanian: a reference grammar* by L. Newmark and others (1982). Orthography was standardised in 1972.

There is a good two-volume dictionary (Albanian-English and English-Albanian) by G. Kiçi, published on good paper in the U.S.A. and obtainable at £18 the set from Regent Holidays. A much cheaper French-English and English-French dictionary published on appallingly bad newsprint in Tirana can be purchased from Heffer's Bookshop, 21 Trinity St., Cambridge for £4.20 the set of two volumes.

The best tool for learning the colloquial language is *Spoken Albanian*, by Leonard Newmark and others, published in 1980 by Spoken Language Services, Inc., P.O. Box 783, Ithaca, New York 14850 at US$10.00. It is available at £10 from Silco Books, 7 Russell Gardens, London NW11 9NJ. There are six dual-track cassettes at US$60.00, not stocked in the U.K., but ordered on request by air.

If you prefer to study the language in Albania by the direct method, from 1982 Tirana University and Albturist offer a course through Regent Holidays. Departure through Belgrade was on 10 August and return again through Belgrade on 29 August. Except for the nights of 10 and 28 August, accommodation was in a twin-bedded room at the Hotel Tirana on full board, the total cost being £415 plus £10.20 insurance, and £6.80 visa. Tuition at Tirana University five mornings a week was supplemented by a choice of excursions.

No language can ever be truly foreign in Europe if the word for book is 'libër', but there are some surprises, like *motrë*, sister not mother. The order of the words resembles English more than German, and numerous words stand out as immediate borrowings from Italian, Greek, Turkish, or the Slav family—even French and English. So the following need no introduction from me, Albanian as they are: fanatik, ju ('j' pronounced like English 'y'), restorant, sërvitor, radio, mozaike, festivali, industrial, agjencia, gjimnastika, televizion, ekonomike, and so on.

To enable you to pronounce the words you see in the Albturist *Handbook of English-Albanian Conversation* (Tirana, 1972), still on sale for 2 leks at the Hotel Adriatiku, Durrës in mid-1982, here is a guide to the consonants and vowels which differ from those in English:

a	*a* in c*a*lm
c	*ts* in ca*ts*
ç	*ch* in *ch*ur*ch*
dh	*th* in *th*e
ë	*e* in th*e*
gj	*g* in *g*uess followed instantly by *y* in *y*es, as in *g*ewgaw
j	*y* in *y*es
ll	*l* in bott*l*e
nj	*n* in *n*et followed instantly by *y* in *y*es, as in *n*ews
q	almost impossible for an English-speaking person to master: try the opening two sounds of *K*ew, with a trace of *ch* in *ch*urch and even a suspicion of *ts* in ca*ts*
rr	The Italian trilled *r* as in ca*rr*ozza
sh	*sh* in *sh*ort, but remember it is one letter of the alphabet, and thus you look it up in a dictionary after *syze* (spectacles), just as *dh, gj, ll, nj, rr, th, xh* and *zh* are treated as one letter of the alphabet, and come respectively after *d, g, l, n, r, t, x,* and *z*
th	*th* as in *th*ink, not *th*ose
x	*dz* as in wor*ds*
y	The French *u* in t*u* or German *u* umlaut in *ü*ber
zh	*zh* as in lei*s*ure

Words and Phrases

Excuse me! (To one person)	Me fal!
(To more than one)	Me falni!
Don't mention it!	S'ka perse!
Hello!	Tungjatjeta!

Yes	Po (shake head)
No	Jo (nod head)
Please (To one person)	Të lutem
(To more than one)	Ju lutem
Thanks (To one person)	Të falemnderit
(To more than one)	Ju falemnderit
How are you?	Si jeni?
Not too bad	Jo aq keq
Very well thanks	Shumë mirë, falemnderit
Not so well	Jo aq mirë
So-so	Ashtu ashtu
Good morning!	Mirë mengjesi!
Good day!	Diten e mirë!
Good evening!	Mirëmbrema!
Good night!	Naten e mirë!
Goodbye!	Mirupafshim!
I am sorry	Më vjen keq
This	Ky (m.); kjo (f.)
That	Atë (m.); ajo (f.)
How much/is...? are...?	Sa/kushton...? kushtoj...?
O.K.	Mirë
It is expensive	Eshtë i shtrënjtë
Where is...?	Ku është...?
Where are...?	Ku janë...?
A little, not much	Pak
Very, much, many	Shumë
All, none	Të gjithë, asnji
Wait! (To one person)	Prit!
(To more than one)	Pritni!
Come here! (To one person)	Eja këtu!
(To more than one)	Ejani këtu!
Go away! (To one person)	Ik!
(To more than one)	Ikni!
Have you...?	A keni...?
Bring me...! (To one person)	Sillmë...!
(To more than one)	Sillmëni...!
What is your name?	Si (How) ju (you) quajnë (they name)?
My name is...	Emri (The name) im (my) është (is) ...
Pleased to meet you	Gëzohem t'ju njoh
This is my friend ...	Ky është miku im ...

Where are you from?	Nga kemi ardhur?
We come from England	Kemi ardhur nga Anglia
May I help you with something?	Mund (May) t'ju ndihmoj (you-I-help) me (with) gjëkafshë (something)?
We should like to meet some Albanians	Duam të takojmë ca shqiptarë
Don't be shy!	Mos (Don't) ki turp!
Finally we are in Tirana	Me në fund, jemi në Tiranë
I know	Njoh
Walk straight to the mosque, then turn right	Ec (pl. Ecni) drejt xhamisë, pastaj (then) kthehu djathtas
We couldn't find it	Nuk mund ta gjenim
Not at all	Hiç
Nothing at all	Hiçasgjë
Do you understand me?	A më kuptoni?
I don't understand you	S'të kuptoj
Slowly; quickly	Ngadalë; shpejt
Please speak more slowly	Ju lutem, flisni më ngadalë
To the right; on the right	Djathtas; në anën e djathtë
To the left; on the left	Majtas; në anën e majtë
Bread; meat; fish	Bukë; mish; peshk
Beer; water; wine	Birrë; ujë; verë
Tea; coffee; milk	Çaj; kafe; qumësht
Potatoes; tomatoes	Patate; dhomate
Eggs; butter; sugar	Vezë; gjalpë; sheqer
Breakfast; lunch; dinner	Bukë mëngjesi; drekë; darkë
Do you speak Albanian?	A dini shqip?
Only a little	Vetëm pak
Do you speak English?	A flisni anglisht?
Hotel; restaurant	Hotel; restorant
A single room	Një dhomë për nji vetë
A double room	Një dhomë për dy veta
Write it on the bill	Shkruje në hesap
I should like my key	Dua çelesin timë
Where is the toilet?	Ku është nevojtorja?
And; but	E, dhe; po, por
Can you (sg.) tell me where the post office is?	A mund të më thuash ku është posta?
Can you (pl.) tell me where there is a hospital?	A mund të më thoni ku ka një spital?

161

Numbers

1	një		9	nentë
2	dy		10	dhjetë
3	tre (*f.* tri)		11	njëmbedhjetë, etc.
4	katër		20	njëzet, etc.
5	pesë		100	njëqind, etc.
6	gjashtë		1,000	mijë
7	shtatë		2,000	dy mijë, etc.
8	tetë		1st	i pari (*f.* e para)

Days and Months

Sunday	e dielë		January	kallnuer (or janar)
Monday	e henë		February	fruer (or shkurt)
Tuesday	e martë		March	mars
Wednesday	e mërkurë		April	prill
Thursday	e enjtë		May	maj
Friday	e premtë		June	qershor
Saturday	e shtunë		July	korrik
			August	gusht
			September	shtator
			October	tetor
			November	nëntor
			December	dhjetor

Official Holidays and Festivals

Christmas, Easter, Ramadan and 'Id al-Fitr are no longer permitted festivals in atheist Albania. Here are the official days of public rejoicing:

January 1	New Year's Day
January 11	Proclamation of the Republic
May 1	May Day
November 7	Victory of the October Socialist Revolution
November 28	Proclamation of Independence
November 29	Liberation Day, 1944

Books and Maps

Most of the books on Albania are in Albanian, and have never been translated: the vast majority date from the last forty years, and consequently show only the official Communist view to the exclusion of balance, a stigma attaching to the otherwise quite readable *History of Albania* by S. Pollo and A. Puto (Routledge, 1981). A far more balanced view is offered by Anton Logoreci in *The Albanians* (Gollancz, 1977 o.p.; Westview Press, 5500 Central Avenue, Boulder, Colo. 80301, 1978) for the modern period. In French we have *L'Albanie* by Georges Castellan (Presses Universitaires de France, 1980), brief but reliable. The most comprehensive works are the outdated *Albania* (British Admiralty, 1945) and the *Area Handbook for Albania* (American University, 1971), for all Albanian publications are heavily censored, omitting what is considered 'sensitive' or 'classified' at that particular time. Thus, *L'agriculture dans la Republique Populaire Socialiste d'Albanie* (Tirana, 1981) is statistically useless because data are never given in absolute terms, but only relative to the base year of 1938.

Town plans are obviously prepared for internal consumption, but are not available in bookshops or hotels. Thus, the latest published town plans of Tirana, Durrës, Sarandë, Shëngjin, Vlorë, Elbasan and Shkodër are in the Admiralty handbook cited above and date probably to 1944, since when an earthquake has devastated Shkodër (1979), and urban renewal has transformed the centre of Tirana.

The folding map of Albania produced in Tirana and on sale in the Albanian shop in London at £1.00 has been superseded by the 1981 country map reproduced in the present book, showing new roads and railways. I strongly recommend two low-priced atlases produced for Albanian schools and available in most bookshops: *Atlas Histori e Shqipërisë* (Albanian historical atlas, 4 leks, Tirana, 1972) and *Atlas për Klasën IV të ciklit të ulët të shkollës 8-vjeçare* (Atlas for the fourth class of the lower range of the 8-year school, 3½ leks, Tirana, 1980).

The best source of books from and about Albania in the U.K. is The Albanian Society, 26 Cambridge Road, Ilford, Essex (tel. 01–590 9977), run by W.B. Bland. Mr. Bland is not only highly knowledgeable about Albania, but is particularly friendly to those willing to study Albania with an open mind. He imports books from Albania, as does The Albanian Shop, Betterton St., near Covent Garden. This shop also sells wine, food, records, and handicrafts: it is located in the basement of The Gramophone Exchange, and is currently open only during weekday afternoons.

In the U.S.A. the best source for information on Albania is Jack Shulman, P.O. Box 912, New York, N.Y. 10008, editor of the irregular *Albania Report*. The *Report* is a useful mouthpiece for the Albanian-language press in the face of monolithically hostile American journalism about Albania. Subscriptions to the *Report* are not solicited, but donations are invited, $10.00 securing an almost complete set. Dozens of books and English-language magazines are imported and made available at a very moderate cost. For instance, the 1977 Constitution costs 50c plus 40c postage, and Arben Puto's *From the Annals of British Diplomacy* costs $1.50 plus 75c postage.

 Index

166